COMATIZED

Part two

Continued

by
Missy C. Luckett

1

Printed by CreateSpace, an Amazon.com company.

ISBN-13:978-1507664902
ISBN-10:1507664907

Individual sales may be purchased at
Missy's "Out of the Way" Cafe.
860 Horseshoe bend road
Raywick, Kentucky. 40060

ACKNOWLEDGMENTS:

TO ALL THE PEOPLE IN THIS CIRCUS!
Illustration: compliments of Summer Luckett

CONTENTS

INTRODUCTION-RECAP

Lets start out with a quote---- *"The secret of change is to focus all of your energy, not on fighting the old, but on building the new"--Socrates---*

With that being said, I'm reclaiming bits and pieces of my life, I guess by telling you about my life and the people in it.

FYI 1: I'm not an adjective kinda girl.

FYI 2: None of these stories need to be embellished, if anything I've toned them down to save the feelings of others.

FYI 3: I fear the grammar police. (AKA Nicole)

FYI 4: It's just life.

FYI 5: If you can't find the humor in it, you haven't dealt with it yet.

OKAY READERS: Welcome back! It's been awhile.

Maybe you read my first book or maybe you didn't. I would recommend reading it, just so you don't get lost. My first story was written about different segments of my life, and so is this one. It begins with my path of growing up in Raywick, then skipping to the middle of my life when tragedy hit and explaining the crazy things before and after the fire. My writings started out as a healing process or these stories never would have been written. Someone read them and told me to make it into a book. So I did, and while writing, and after hitting sixty-thousand words for the first one, I realized I could never get all my stories into one book. Just impossible, too many places, too many stories and too many interesting people. With that being said, this has been a planned series ever since.

Every time I try to go back and write a story, a new one comes about, so it's very hard to stay focused on what I started. Every mile I travel has a unique story about the people in my life. Literally every curve of these country roads and beyond, bring back a funny, exciting or terrifying story.

So let the saga continue, as I put myself on the line and out there for your entertainment. I'm just wanting to record my experiences, and maybe let you readers laugh and feel. Just know that when I start to fall down the rabbit hole, into the unexpected terrain, I try not to panic. I've learned over the years to treat things like an adventure instead of a crisis, just like Alice in Wonderland. So if you feel the waters are getting too deep, just know I will pull you up before you lose a breath. Well, you might lose one or two, so be very quiet little rabbit, and see the shit I have, cause I've seen a lot.

So, lets go about it like this, like a TV series and update you on what happened last season in a flash, or faster than you can smack a tick. Maybe not that fast, but you get what I'm saying.

Mom and Dad had sex in the back of a car, thence was my creation. I attended their shotgun wedding, Yes! Still in the womb. They moved me to several locations, tried to burn me, then drown me, not on purpose of course, but true.

Then Mom and Dad got a divorce while I was a toddler. Yes, I came from what some people would call a broken home, but I don't look at it that way. Keep in mind, divorce is not a bad thing, it's just not settling for less than you want. Don't know who didn't want what, and I've never really asked. I really don't need to know, don't need to dredge things up. Obviously something went wrong way back when, and I'm sure fingers could get pointed, cause no one ever wants to take the blame. Now do they? The way I look at it, they were too young to be married and maybe didn't want to just coexist.

At age five, I moved to my Moms hometown, (Raywick) to live with my grandparents and Uncle Robbie. I experienced tragedy at a young age when we lost our dear cousin Jojo, at the of age of ten, to an accident.

I also introduced you to my crazy uncle Charlie, who is a true Raywickian. I told stories of my grandma and her crazy wit and her old time pranks. Familiarized you with my uncle Jimmy who was involved with the *Cornbread Mafia* and spent 20 years in prison. I moved around some more, went to college, then had my baby girl. Moved to a farm house out in bum f*ck, on the outskirts of Raywick and called it my last and final destination. Then I opened my Cafe, out in this neck of the woods. Which I'm gonna elaborate on in this story. Last, but not least, I watched my house burn to the ground on Halloween Day 2008. I left you with a thought, "MAYBE." I'm

8

looking for answers and I hope we can find the answers together. The investigation is on, even though I know that most stories really don't have absolute closure, but we will see.

Summer and me. Last picture taken inside our home that burnt. Impression of Robert Palmer.

Before we look for some of the answers, let's rewind and see how this domino effect came into play. I will introduce you to some more interesting people who have come in and out of my life. I'm not sure of all the dates and times when all the people came rolling through, but I will try to keep a somewhat efficient time line. Once again, we will not concern ourselves too much with it.

I want to continue this series, so that I can figure out how to let go of the life I had planned, and be willing to accept the life that is waiting for me. This is a process, trying to figure out the mysteries of my world and my surroundings and the changes that constantly have to be adapted to. I honestly can't finish one story without another story happening simultaneously. But while writing this, not only have I realized that life automatically make changes for us, I also realize we should make changes for ourselves more often. Sometimes we seem to get stuck in the same day to day activity. We are not like salmon, we don't have to always swim upstream, we don't always have to stay in the same direction. We can change our course at any time. You can swim up and down that river as many times as you want, till you find what you're looking for. You can even head off into the crevices in search for something different. You just have to watch out for bears, they will get you and eat you, and that would be an unexpected occurrence, just like a lot of these stories.

So here we go, I would like to take you back to the custody battle. It was soon after the death of my cousin Jojo. We were both ten at the time when he lost his precious life.

I will try to make this segment short and sweet. Although nothing about my life has been short and sweet. Sometimes I feel as if the Sour Patch Kids have invaded my space. Luckily for me, I have learned to chew them up, swallow the sweet, then spit out the sour.

10

Hence, came the word Comatized to me. Don't let the bitter leave a nasty taste in your mouth.

I'm sure to skip many stories, adventures, and mishaps. I will let you in on them in the near future, but for now I would like to get you back up to date on what's going on here, on this plantation, that I still call home, even though something or someone, wanted me gone by burning down the house.

Quote: *We are all lying in the gutter, but some of us are looking at the stars." - Oscar Wilde -*

☆ ON THE MOVE AGAIN

Here I was at age ten, still living in Raywick, where the farm animals outnumber the residents. There is not a red light to be found for miles and miles. I remember standing on my uncle Louis Earl's carport talking to my Grandma. His house was a stone's throw from Grandma and sat across from the old gas station I used to run to, to fetch gas. Grandma would hand me a jug and a quarter and it would fill it up. Yep! Gasoline was a quarter a gallon back in those days.

Louis Earl and Grandma

Louis Earl's house also sat beside this old barn that some man had hung himself in. Not sure why the man hung himself, lots of speculation on that. My Uncle Charlie was one of the first persons on the scene and drew an illustration of the man hanging there. He published the picture in his book 'Raywickians.'

It was spooky as hell walking past it as a young child. It always felt as if someone was peeking through the cracks, just waiting for you to be curious or stupid enough to walk in. Glad curiosity didn't kill the cat on this one. I'm adventurous, just not that brave to stroll in alone. It has been torn down since my younger days and now it is a cute little park, for all the little Raywickians to play in.

I knew my Mom and Dad had been discussing my dad's intentions of getting custody of me. I don't remember or think there was a hearing, or what the reasons were that he was removing me from Raywick. I have heard rumors, but we will just leave it at that, RUMORS. Pretty sure it was another mutual agreement, on both my parent's part and not actually a war, but then again, surely I was worth at least a battle. But there was no battle, because it became my choice, yes, I got a choice, I think.

I remember my grandma asking. "Honey, you don't want to move with your Dad, do ya? Don't you like it here?"

All I could think inside my head was... "Yes ma'am I do." I was thinking yes ma'am, because we had been scolded before, if we didn't use the word ma'am. No words were really coming out of my teeny tiny mouth. I just stood there in silence.

"Missy!" She said, "Are you wanting to go with your Dad?"

She startled me back to attention and at that point, I realized that maybe the final decision was mine. I didn't want to hurt her feelings, because I loved her dearly. But yet, I blurted out. "Yes ma'am, I do." Why? What's in it for me? Kids! I wanted to be where all the kids were. Kids, kids, and more kids. On top of that, my own television, that's all I could think. If I had lots of kids around I was gonna be happier than a biscuit in gravy, and that there my friends is about as happy as you can get in the country. Especially if they're made by Grandma, boy was I gonna miss those homemade biscuits and gravy.

The only thing I remember after that, is my dad picking me up and driving me to his mother's house. You know, the maw-maw I would visit on the weekends. He dropped me off at that brick house that was in the middle of everything exciting, but sad to say, no homemade biscuits and gravy. I had traded that in for nasty

13

grapefruit and raw bacon. Yuk! Well, is wasn't raw, but barely cooked, is close enough. But, that's the way Daddy's mom liked it.

I was on the move again. This would be my sixth relocation in my small life span, you would think I was an army brat. My life was already becoming an after school special, one with adventures and twists. Do they even still make those shows anymore? Speaking of shows, I loved me some *Little Rascals* and *Planet of the Apes* back in those days, and refused to watch cartoons. Weird, I know. While writing this, I'm figuring out I may be a little weirder than I thought. I will let you be the decision maker on that. Like I tell people who are headed to Mardi Gras, just keep an open mind if you want to enjoy yourself.

Yep! That's me and dad looking all cool in the seventies at Maw-maw's during one of my weekend visits.

Just a memory: Mom took me to Louisville one day to see a movie, I was maybe seven or eight at the time. We swung by Kathleen's and picked up little Danny who was a couple years younger than me. She dropped us off at the big Showcase Cinema to see Star Wars. Loved me some Chewbacca. But anyway, when the movie was over there was no one there to pick us up. Do what? So we did what we thought we should do and snuck ourselves into another movie. I don't recall the movie or how we were found, but luckily we were. I think she was trying to get me kidnapped, then felt guilty and came back searching for me.

Maw-maw and Aunt Peggy on her wedding day, duh....

My maw-maw, who was seventy was sixty years older than I. That's a huge gap on raising a kid, can you imagine raising a small kid at that age? She always reminded me of *Vicki Lawrence*, who played *Thelma Harper,* on *Mamas Family*. She was quite the comedian and ruled the roost with her wisecracks. Although she wasn't as moody and didn't really insult people or drink Budweiser like Thelma. Never seen her take a drink in my life.

She was a very laid-back woman and my friends loved to come over just to hang out with her, she was just that entertaining and her personality just naturally appealed to people.

One day in the kitchen, my friends and I were sitting at the table. She was still in her nightgown as usual, when she reached in the cabinet to get her a pink snowball to eat. She dropped one on the floor and when she bent over, she let out the biggest fart I had ever heard, right in front of us. Her nightgown literally moved.

All I could say was, "Maw-maw!"

Then we all giggled like it was the funniest thing on earth.

She looked up and said, "I will shit in your face, if I want to."

Well...... We all just busted out in laughter once again, we fell plum out of our chairs.

"But Maw-maw that's rude."

"Is that coming from the book of Who Cares?" she replied.

"Well! I guess if you have to fart you have to fart, but damn! That one peeled our hair back."

"Guess you better be glad I was wearing underwear today or it might have knocked you against the wall."

I know that on her part, that may sound or seem a tad bit rude. But then again, is farting rude, while in the comfort of your own home? But I'm also thinking she just didn't give a shit. Which is fine by me, sometime you have the right to not give a shit.

She was real...... and she didn't give two shits about blurting out whatever was on her mind. She was a 'tell-it-like-it-is-kind-of-lady. Other than being just plain ass comical, she was honest and upfront as hell. She knew how to keep me honest too, for the most part.

My friends today still talk about her. They say that woman was aware of everything, I mean everything going on around her. They said it was hilarious when she would talk about people not being very smart, and saying that they didn't know the difference between shit and apple butter. Wouldn't she be amazed with the era of smart phones and stupid people.

I never saw her smoke or drink, but boy, was she addicted to Vicks Salve. She would take that stuff with her finger and stuff it right in her nose. That was some serious nasty mentholated goop. The smell of that shit would fill up the whole room. I just couldn't take it and would have to exit the building, I don't know how she did it.

Maw-maw and Grand-paw had already raised all eleven kids, before she took on me. She had twelve, but her youngest died as an infant. He had a hole in its lung, which in these days, that would be fixable, but back then, not so much.

Maw-maw and Grandpa and all their chitlins.
Just some stupid things her chitlins did:

My dad's brothers and sisters use to stuff their sister Darlene, in the mailbox, obviously she was a little fart. (bottom far left) When Peggy (sitting in maw-maw's lap) would get lucky enough to get a bottle of Coke, she would take only a few drinks because she wanted to make it last. She never knew when her next one would come. So to make sure no one else drank it, she would put a rubber band around it to mark it, then stick it in the fridge. She thought somehow she would know if someone had taken a drink. Not knowing that some of her brothers and sisters were smart enough to take a drink and roll it right on down, but they knew that they couldn't be tempted to take the last drink or they would be caught. Poor Peggy, she was never none the wiser back then. Guess that's why Maw-maw use to tell her kids, if they all put their brains together, it would still

19

only equal one of hers. In a joking manner of course, but still called you out for not being very smart, when the opportunity arose.

My dad, (in between Grandpa's legs) accidentally killed one of his daddy's pigs. He told me he was trying to get it out of the pond. So he came up with a hair brained idea and decided to just throw a rock at it. He said it hit her right in the head, right between the eyes and it sunk, straight down it went. When he came home without the pig, he got his butt kicked. How the hell he killed a pig with a rock amazes me, you can hardly kill those tough things with a bullet. Guess that's why he got to end up playing baseball, or maybe the fact, he made a deal with his Dad. A sneaky deal at that. Story goes, Pawpaw had lost his wallet. My dad asked his Dad, if I find it, can I play ball? His Dad said, yes, of course son. So they sealed the deal with spit and a hand shake. Dad being sneaky and already knowing where it was, went and ran it through the dirt and mud. He brought it back to the house and acted like he found it in the field. Grandpa was none the wiser and that sure enough, that deal landed him on the baseball team for two years. Sometimes a kids gotta do what a kids gotta do.

Darlene said, she caught the house on fire twice and wrecked two tractors.

I've also heard that Dad use to stick communion in his pocket because he didn't like it. Almost every Sunday Maw-maw would have to take his shirt off and take it back up to church and give it to the priest. Why take the whole shirt? Because back then you wasn't suppose to touch the communion.

Daddy also got drug through the field by Grandpa's tractor plow. They said it tore his face all up, kinda like I did mine when riding my bike. We both should look a little bit like Scarface, but we don't, not yet anyway.

Aunt Libby (far right front row) said she was happy to get a sandwich once a week. Why a sandwich? Because she got tired of eating steak and good stuff like that. She said, boy! Daddy really did take good care of us, but that sandwich sure did taste good. Aunt Libby also had polio growing up. Frankie (hiding between Mawmaw and Grandpa) said she would always bring books home from school, homework or no homework. Why? Because her dad would always say, anyone who doesn't have homework has to help with the chores. So, to her, carrying books home was always worth the hassle. She said, don't think I ever had to do a chore.

Oh, let's rewind for a second and fast forward at the same time. I forgot to tell you that my dad about burnt the house down out in Rolling Hills. You know, the house I used to escape from, when I was around three or four. You would only know this if you read part one. He supposedly fell asleep while smoking a cigarette. Fire has been at my heels for as long as I can remember. For now, I keep escaping its wrath, but I'm beginning to wonder what the common denominator is. Don't worry, I got a few things and people in mind. Wink, wink.

REAL TIME conversation: Darlene telling me about the fire at my first book signing.
She was telling me she lived in the neighborhood, near me when I was just a toddler. She said Mom came running down there screaming. "The house is on fire! The house is on fire! Buddy won't get out of the house." She said "When we drove back up there, the fire department was boarding it up." Then Darlene asked me, "Where were you, Missy?" I just laughed and said, "Oh Darlene, I

21

was probably already at a neighbor's house. The question is, where was Daddy?"

Then I told Darlene that Miss Ewing, the person's house whom I was probably at, had just left my book signing. She was telling me that Mom used to come running over there with Daddy chasing her. Darlene must have misunderstood me, because she asked. "How did Mrs. Ewing know Momma? I never saw her and daddy ever get into an argument." I laughed, "no Darlene, I mean my mom and dad." She replied, "Oh, I thought you meant my mom and dad. The only thing I ever saw Daddy do, was get up from the table and pitch a tea towel on Momma, they never fought."

All I could think was "WOW!" Now that was a Mr. and Mrs. Cleaver situation.

Maw-maw and Grandpa

Just wanted to let you know a little bit about my Dad's family. They are definitely worthy of being talked about, just maybe a little too normal to write about. Born, grew up, married, had kids, BAM. And that my friends, is why there aren't or won't be many stories about my dad's family. It's sad to say, but you can't tell many stories about how well a family gets along, now is there? Well, '*Leave it to*

Beaver' made it work. But they didn't have *Fifty Shades of Grey* back then. Just a different crowd to appease to these days, that's all I'm saying. Dad and Peggy might be an exception to the rule, but for now we will keep a long story short and just fast forward. Get back to Dad and Peggy in the near future.

Back into the main story. Since I had relocated, I had to start a new school. It was a Catholic school. I was required to wear navy blue uniforms and I wasn't happy about it. I like my street clothes, but I had to buy new ones, well I didn't buy them, per say. Although we could wear slacks, my maw-maw had also bought me a couple skirts. I was dreading the day I had to put them on. That first night before school and the dreaded skirt wearing, I had a nightmare. I dreamt I was playing kickball at school and forgot to wear my panties. When I went to kick the ball my little cookie was just out there for every one to see. It was plum awful. I woke up in a serious sweat and thought I was gonna die. At that time, it seemed to be the worst thing that could happen to me. But as I have lived and learned, not so much. There are way bigger catastrophes lurking out there among us, like the Loch Ness Monster, Bigfoot and Jaws.

Anyway, the new school sat on the same street as Maw-maw's. You know the main highway leading into town. This school was also within walking distance. I walked that familiar route for four years, come rain or shine.

I remember my first day of school when I strutted into the room, rocking my new blue skirt. The teacher tried to get me to sit with this girl who had long blonde hair and had it in a pony tail. I didn't know her from Adam and I kinda shook my head and said. "Nah.....I don't wanna." As I spotted Julie. Yeah, yeah, yeah, I know her. "I will sit with her." I said. Julie was the first friend I made when I would visit Maw-maw. I use to always play with her on the weekends, she was

24

an active child like me, we got into all kinds of mischief together. So I walked over to her desk. "Scoots over." Then we wiggled in the chair together. We were both grinning ear to ear.

So now we were gonna get to be best buddies everyday. Why was I having to sit with someone? Not sure, no extra desk for the new kid, I think. How bold was I to tell the teacher 'NO' on my first day of school. GO ME!

Julie and I used to ride our bikes together out in Rolling Hills, back in the day when you could still do that kind of stuff without adult supervision. Except when you're three, that shit will get you in trouble. It also makes Houdini show up and make your bike disappear. It wasn't long before Julie and I got in our first argument. I don't even remember what it was about. I told you previously I don't like controversy and I don't. I mean we were literally ready to kick each other's butts over something, I recall the argument going something like this.

"Missy, you better meet me at the Junior High tomorrow morning at nine and I'm gonna kick your butt."

"Shut your face Julie, we will see about that." I screamed back at the top of my lungs and then ran off.

It must have been during summer break, because days went by, before I saw Julie again. I was really starting to miss her. When we finally went back to school, I asked her. "Where were you the day you were gonna beat me up?"

"I was at the school."

In a very smart ass tone I replied back, "Oh really! Where, at the school?"

Her voice got louder. "Round front by the tree, waiting for you. Where were you?"

I yelled back, "Oh really, well.....I was on the other side."

She pointed at me, "No you weren't."

My voice was starting to tremble. "Yes I was!"

I was trying to stand my ground. While knowing.... I wasn't there at all. I lied. Why was I not there? For starters, I wasn't going to fight my best friend Julie, but I didn't want to back down like a little sissy either. Even though I didn't go.

So, we kept going back and forth. Finally, I was like, "Julie, I didn't go at all, because I didn't want to fight you. You're my best friend."

"Well, Missy, I didn't go either."

As we both laughed with relief. "You wanna go ride bikes after school?" she asked.

"Sure!"

So when the bell rang, off to the hills we went riding bikes till dark and coming home looking like little dust monkeys. We never tried to fight each other again.

Me, Julie, don't know and Michelle

26

Julie and I liked to go to her room and pretend we could sing and yes I said pretend. Our favorite singing act was from the movie and album *Grease.* We would stand in front of the mirror and blurt out the song. Honestly we should have been lip syncing instead, we weren't the best. I'm sure we sounded like some tied up hound dogs.

I would sing *John Travolta's* lines, and she would sing *Olivia Newton Johns* lines. Even though I'm the one who looked more like Olivia, because of course, I had the blonde hair. I sang John's lines, because my voice was deeper and I sounded more like him. I still love those songs. Summer even likes that old time musical, it is vintage. *Tell me more, tell me more, was it love at first sight. Tell me more, tell me more, did she put up a fight....... Those sum---mer niiiiiggggghhhhts.*

Somewhere during all this, my Dad had bought a house out near Jesse Town. He was definitely living in the seventies. He had wall paper in his living room that sported a huge ass river scene. I have never seen anything like that in anyone's home, ever! His closet was filled with disco shirts and of course he had the side burns to match the time. He also had one of those big wooden box stereos filled with disco music. He would occasionally take Julie and I out there to stay all night. We would scavenge through his old albums, we thought we hit the jackpot when we discovered the album, *Saturday Night Fever.* The Bee Gees and John were the shit back in those days. We would put on his shirts and strut through the house singing: *"Oh you can tell by the way I use my walk I'm a woman's man, no time to talk."* I'm sure you know the rest. Hope you catch yourself singing it the rest of the day. Don't be mad at me, when you do.

Oh and he had a water bed. Cool Huh? Not to me, because most of the time I was afraid to sleep in it. Why? Because, freakin' Jaws was going to get me. Literally, I thought that.

This was in the eighties and the fabulous wallpaper at dad's.

SUCKEN ON POPSICLES

It wasn't long before I started to make new friends and Julie kinda slipped off the radar for a moment. Not sure how that happened. Maybe because I started hanging out with my second cousin Marybeth who lived four houses up the street from Maw-maw. I didn't play with her much when I was younger, I mean younger younger. She was a girly girl, and would cry when we played kick ball and the ball would hit her or something stupid like

28

that. I mean, what a whiny baby! That's why I liked playing with Julie, she was rough and tough like me. We didn't cry when we got hit by a plastic ball. I didn't even cry the day my cousin Garland started chasing me around the house at my aunt's. I was running as fast as I could. I looked back to see how far away he was, and when I turned back around, low and behold there was an air conditioner sticking out of the window. Not sure where it came from, but BAM! Took my feet right out from under me and I saw stars. Someone picked me up as blood was running in my eyes and took me in the house to bandage me up, no stitches, no cry. It left another scar down the side of my nose, right beside the scar Robbie had caused just a few years earlier. So now I was sporting my third scar. This body is made for scarring and that's just what I'll do, I will keep scarring this body, till my time is due.

Back to Marybeth, even though she was still a girly girl and a momma's girl. She ended up being one of my best friends. Lifetime friend. She had dark hair with caterpillar eyebrows. When she smiled, dimples pressed into her pretty face. Let's say she was very cute and petite. Happy to say, she still is today. Not that it matters to me how pretty she is, but I'm sure she is happy about it.

One day while down my house, Maw-maw caught Marybeth gazing at herself in the storm door. Maw-maw busted her out right away and called her a little prissy butt. She was quite prissy. If there was a selfie stick back then, she would have been sure to use it, over and over again. My cousin Jeff, Darlene's son, didn't like playing ball with her or my cousin Ann. Ann lived in Fern Creek and was my uncle Tommy's daughter. She use to play in the back yard with dolls instead. Even when we would get her to play, she wouldn't let Jeff pitch to her, think he hit her a time or two. Jeff would tell her to go back and play with her dolls. He would call her a sissy and he

29

nicknamed Marybeth, hairy breath. Marybeth hated it with a passion. So in return she would yell back at him, cracker feet. Why? Because his feet always smelled like wet crackers. I know what you're thinking, what do wet crackers smell like? Well! Go stick some in water and find out. It's not the most pleasant smell, but then again, I've smelled worse, even tasted worse, but still stinky all the same. Anybody ever watch *Bizarre Foods* with *Andrew Zimmerman?* It makes me cringe when he eats things, then describes it tasting like iodine, fish butt and even Grand-paw's sweater. Then I realize those cracker feet just don't seem all that bad anymore.

It's just the simple things you remember sometimes. You know, back when a hoe was a hoe. Coke was a coke, and crack's what you were doing, when you were cracking jokes. I miss back when. Thanks *Tim McGraw,* I like that song, and the simple times too.

Let's talk about Peggy, my dad's younger sister. I guess at this time she was in her mid twenties and sported blazing bright red hair, glasses and had snowy white skin with freckles. She was living in Louisville at the time when I first moved in with Maw-maw. But she and her son Travis would soon come too. That boy was only four, but a mean little shit. They would take up residence in the basement. The one I had previously almost been burnt up in as a baby.

One hot summer day, Marybeth and I were walking from her house with popsicles. Travis and Peggy were outside at Maw-maw's. Travis wanted one, but we had none to spare. He started kicking and screaming, "I want one! I want one! You better give me one!"

We told him we had no more. Then he threw his big Tonka truck at Marybeth and hit her in the leg. She was hobbling around and about to cry, when Aunt Peggy came over and started fussing shaking her finger in our face. "What is wrong with you girls?

Coming down here in front of Travis, sucking on those popsicles like you're sucking on your Momma's titties."

While at the time, we were both scared of Travis and Aunt Peggy, we couldn't help but giggle and whisper to each other. "Sucking on your momma's titties."

As Aunt Peggy grabbed Travis's arm sternly. "Come on Travis, I will go get you a popsicle. You don't need to be around these titty babies."

I mean damn.....Aunt Peggy! We were kids too. Who says shit like that? Aunt Peggy and Uncle Charlie, that's who.

After that, Marybeth, was even more afraid of Travis, even though he was just a toddler, she thought he was mean as a rattlesnake. But he really put a hurting on her with that truck. He was a mean.... little fart. Guess like my uncle Charlie when he was a kid. Maybe we all have one of those in our lifetime. I heard rumors my dad was a mean little shit too. But he turned out to be friendlier than *Casper the Friendly Ghost*, himself.

Marybeth is married with a family now and lives in Saint Louis. I was just on the phone with her the other day when I brought up the popsicle story. She stated she use to be afraid of Peggy.. And I was like, "I know this. What about Travis?" As I giggled.

"Yep, I's scared of him too." As we busted out laughing.

Yep, that's Travis.

Quick story: *My aunt Peggy told me a story about Travis biting Daddy on the butt, while he was frying bacon in his Fruit of the Looms. Now that takes talent and guts.*

At night, when it was time for Marybeth to go home, she hated with a passion to make the walk back home alone. Why? Because in between our homes, sat this old rundown house. It had boarded up windows and seemed inhabited by someone unknown. Maybe looked a little like the house in the movie, *To Kill A Mocking Bird.* You just wanna throw rocks at it and run.

Her mom, would have to meet her at the edge of that old house and I would walk her to my side of it. So after we had split the walk half way, she would see her mom, and would dart past that spooky old house faster than *Forest Gump.* Run Forest run. Then I would turn and run back home just as fast. Naw! Let's go with faster, I was faster than Marybeth. My maw-maw was too old and couldn't get around well enough to walk me. So I was on my own.

It was sometime in the summer of 1979 when my dad and Jackie (a gentleman who helped him sell cars) took Marybeth and I to see our first real scary movie. *Amittyville Horror,* it scared the crap out of us. It put fear in us for a long, long time, even today. But if you read the first book, you already know this. Some of those movies are just hard to shake.

After getting to see that movie, Marybeth and Shannon, stayed all night with me. Of course Maw-maw was attending bingo, for the one-millionth time. We ended up watching another scary movie called *Halloween.* Most people know about this infamous movie and if you don't, you have been living in a cave. While watching it, we realized it had an old house that looked just like the one we had been running past. The house became even scarier than before. It was *Michael Myers* house, yikes!!!! Scary! We were really scared now. We also picked out who we were gonna be in the movie, just to make it more interesting and exciting. Damn if I didn't pick the girl that got killed first, BAM BOOM! I was DEAD, first murder scene. Should have seen that one coming. She lay there in the bed with just a sheet over her. Obviously she was naked, the first naked lady on

TV that we had seen. Then she pulled out her ta-ta's and said, do you see anything you like? Then Poof! She was gone. It scared the living daylights out of us. Thanks to that movie, it was the first set of ta-ta's I had seen, besides Maw-maws humongous knockers. My friends and I sure weren't rocking any yet. He killed her with the phone cord. Who knew that was a deadly weapon? He couldn't have done that with an iPhone. Thanks *Apple* for lowering statistics of death by phone cords.

So after watching that scary ass movie, Maw-Maw, Peggy and I were in the kitchen one evening, right as night began to fall. I looked out the window and spotted movement. "Oh shit! Come here you guys." They ran toward the window, well Maw-maw didn't run, she hobbled. We found ourselves staring at a man, staring at us. He was lurking behind the bush on the other side of the driveway. It was just like what Michael would do in the movie. Just standing there tall, broad and stiff. I was scared shitless. We called the law, but when they arrived the man had slipped off into the night, never to be seen again. I think of him sometimes, he is one of those memories that got sizzled in.

Halloween is still my favorite movie and holiday to this day. Don't know why, just is. Maybe I like being spooked. Maybe I'm a spook junky. I mean, whose house burns down on Halloween Day? MINE! It's crazy, I know! You would think that I would hate everything about it.

These are some of the cousins I got to play with while at Maw-maws. Trust me there were a lot more, but these were my neighborhood buddies. From bottom left- Dana, happy happy. Then me, with my one and only pink doll, just happy as a lark. Jeff, hum! You look puzzled. Kevin, looking all mysterious and Marcy, thinking, hey you're cute! Second row, Ann, looking like she seen a ghost. Lori, why so sad? Jamie, posing for school pictures and Garland, trying to get away. Third row, don't know, don't know. Kerry, half head. Joey, seems happy, but I think he is pinching Garlands butt. Then last but not least, Lydia. I have lots of stories about these buddies, but in due time.

Fourth grade------fifth grade

My perms finally started growing out and I never received another after moving out of Grandma's. I've had many random and crazy hairdos like most people, but there's one thing worse. Have you ever met those people who have had the same hair cut since their first grade picture? What's up with that? Fear of change?

I also found a picture with my cousin Dana and Kristi, Darlene's two girls. Kristi being the itty bitty one. She was small like her mom, but I don't think we ever put her in a mailbox. I'm sure we were at one of Dad's softball games.

THE MYSTERY IS OVER

My friend Shannon lived way out in the country. So after school she would walk us home, just to have something to do till her mom got off work. Sometimes we would head to Main Street first, to the local soda shop. It set dead in the middle of our little town. Not as little as Raywick of course, but no big city either, but at least we had four red lights. We would sit at the counter on old spinning stools and order a Rocky Road Sunday, a Coke Float or sometimes a Cola in those old fashion soda bottles. But only if we had the money and I was usually the one with it. Sorry Marybeth, you know its true. LOL.

If we were all broke and maybe only had some change in our pockets, we would have to stop at Druthers, where the original *Burger Queen* use to be. We would get water and 25 cent crumbys. If you don't know what they are, they are the little crumbs that fall off the fish when they would fry it. They were quite the yummy treat. Heart attack city, but yummy. My maw-maw use to take me to Druthers every other Sunday to eat at the buffet. Damn their fried zucchini was delicious. Any of you readers remember that?

On the other Sundays, we would go to a local diner and get some homemade food. They had the best damn stuffed peppers ever. I was always disappointed if they didn't have them on the menu that day. My maw-maw loved to eat out and she would take me places all the time. Maybe that's how I got my creative palate and yearning for something different, other than the same ole, same ole, night after night.

Now Grandma, on the other hand. You know, Mom's mom. She never ate out anywhere, she always cooked. Yep! PINTO BEANS. Yes, she cooked plenty of other things, delicious things. She is actually known as one of the best homemade cooks around. Maybe I should put her on one of those cooking shows. You know where they have home cooks compete. Bet she would kick some ass, even at her age. But when she had beans, a dilemma was in order. I remember having to sit at the table for hours on end. She would say, "You're not leaving this table till you finish your dinner young lady." So, I just sat there with my arms crossed staring at Grandma. It was like a Mexican standoff. Did I really think I was gonna win?

Then when it finally got dark, she would tell me to just go to bed if I couldn't eat my dinner. I do believe it's the latest I ever got to stay up while living there. BEANS! I thank you for that, because in my own little way, I did win. Even though I went to bed hungry.

I hate it when kids or adults won't try new and different foods. But let's just be sure about one thing, if they don't like something, they don't like it. In my eyes, their only allowed to say they don't like it if they have tried it. So parents, remember when you're telling your kids to finish their plate, they just may not like it. Why don't you sit down and eat something you don't like. You would never do it, would you? Nope, didn't think so. Sorry, didn't mean to scold you like that. Let's move on.

I ended up loving and playing team sports. Had to get it from the Luckett side, because they literally bleed sports. I played for the Mets for two years and my cousin Jeff played for the Reds. I think my cousin Kevin played for the Astros, not sure. I actually got to be the first girl to pitch a game. I even struck out a kid that had never been struck out before. Hell! I think it's because I was throwing the ball so slow. Who knows, I may have had a spin on it. But what a great moment, for whatever reason. I was paving the way for girls to play.

39

I didn't get to play but two years because the league only went up to the eighth grade and I started late. Hell! I started everything late, even my period. Haha, sorry, TMI. But there were no sports in Raywick, and it took me a while to figure out that they even existed. I didn't even get to go to the local fair or Ham Days which was one of Marion county's biggest community events. I'm not complaining, I'm just stating.

I also started playing basketball in the seventh grade, for the Saint Augustine Cardinals. My dad used to drive me to the game sometimes in his little buggy patrol. It was purple and had multiple horns you could blow, it even had the horn sound from *The Dukes of Hazards*. It was the coolest thing on wheels at the time. I can tell you what wasn't cool, though. It was when I thought I had started my period. I put a big pad on and lost it on the basketball court. Lets just say, no one knew whose it was, until just now! Saint A team mates, the mystery is over. It twas mine.

Got some stories coming up on these girls. Lynn, bottom far left, number 22. Julie third to left, number 10. Me fifth to the left, number 3. Dawn, second row far right and Paula left of her. I have some stories about you other girls later. Don't hold your breath, might take a minute or two, maybe even a book or two to get there, oh, but we will. I will have to get ahold of Michelle number 15, Kathy number 4 and Renee, number 14, just to see what they have to tell.

Playing basketball is how I met Lynn. Marybeth, Lynn and I became inseparable. Then of course there was Shannon, our fourth best friend.

Lynn lived right up the street from Marybeth and right past the Dairy Freeze. We used to always stop there and get ice cream and mini burgers. Shannon of course lived way... way... out in the country. She and Marybeth weren't into sports. But luckily I don't judge people on their ability to play sports, but sometimes I do judge on the amount of nuggets they have in their box. In recent years, I have met people who think they have a twelve piece box. When in

41

fact, when they speak, I realize that they only have two in there, and one with a bite out of it. Put it this way, not very smart.

SMACKED THE SHIT PLUM OUT OF ME

During these next few stories, I'm guessing I'm around the age twelve or thirteen. It was on a hot summer day when I thought it was time for another bike adventure. Without telling Maw-maw, I hopped on my bike and started to make the long haul out toward Shannon's house. I peddled and peddled, first through the projects, down Woodlawn Avenue, then out to the highway. By this time the sweat was rolling in my eyes and the cars were flying by at high speeds. I thought about turning around, but I told my self, self, we can do this. Then I finally arrived at her long winding country road. I was really wondering what I had gotten myself into, when several different dogs came chasing after my bike. My heart rate increased every time it would happen. I would stand up, put my head down and pedal as hard as I could. I pedaled like my life depended on it, I thought I would never make it alive to my destination. I thanked God when I finally spotted her house over upon the hill. I was one tired son-of-a-bitch. My clothes were ringing wet from head to toe. She was standing out in the yard when I whipped it into the driveway. I was an unexpected guest, so she was shocked to see me. Then I just fell over on my bike, as I laid there on the dirty ground gasping for air. She almost had to resuscitate me. I'm sure I was being a little dramatic, but I truly was exhausted from the challenge I had given myself. She was hovering over me, "Missy are you okay, are you? As I gave her a breathy response, "Yeah, Yeah, I'm fine Shannon."

Later that evening, when her mom got home she had to load my bike up and drive me back to town. I just knew I couldn't make the trot back after almost entering unconsciousness, due to all the peddling it took to get there. At least no one took my bike away from me this time. Guess I was a big girl now, riding ten miles on my bike on hilly, curvy dangerous highways and country roads.

Real time: I was just reading this story to Mom. She busted out like she was concerned. "You did what? You, road your bike that far at age 12?" I looked at her like duh! "Hell yeah! I guess so! If I can ride my damn bike down the highway at 3, don't you think I could do it at the age 12.

Shannon, whom is also married with kids, was telling me on the phone today, that I was the only kid that she knew that was already a natural entrepreneur way back when.

She said. "Missy, you used to not eat your lunch, because you wanted to save your money to buy something. So we were sitting in class one day and Miss Wright asked you a question and you didn't know the answer. She yelled, Missy Luckett! Look at you all slumped down in your seat, hair in your eyes and no food in your belly. Why don't you know the answer? She was so mean to you."

As we both started to laugh. "Yep, some teachers were, guess they didn't see my potential. Kinda like that quote, you can't expect a fish to climb a tree."

Shannon was still laughing, "guess not, but they should have. I did. You can't expect every kid to be the same. You weren't just outside the box, you crushed the box and burnt it."

I had to jump in to tell her a story about me running over bunnies while mowing Maw-maws yard one day. "Shannon, listen! Marybeth was standing on the sidewalk watching me mow. Then all of a sudden I hit this bunny, I mean bunny fur flew out everywhere. I thought Marybeth was gonna just die, you know how girly she is, kinda like you. I just laughed at her and kept mowing. It's not that I didn't feel sorry for the little bunnies, but the deed had been done and I had to finish, if I was to get my allowance."

"Yes, you had to have your allowance."

"Oh! And one time I got lucky enough for someone to give me a pet bunny, so Marybeth and I decided to give it a bath, the next day it was dead."

"Sounds like you need to stay away from bunnies Missy, or at least keep them out of the washing machine and out from under lawnmowers."

"Shannon! You know I didn't put it in the washing machine."

"I know Missy, I know."

Oh yeah, by the way readers. Shannon was the one that picked 'Jamie Lee Curtis', in the movie Halloween. We had picked the girls we were gonna be, based on the order of who got home first. It did make the movie way scarier when it was one of our characters being chased by that psycho Michael, then one of us dying. So I was always home first and as you already know, I was dead. She always got home last and so did Jamie in the movie. So, she got bragging rights on surviving and kicking some Michael Myers ass, even if it was pretend. Weird thing though, is that she had a cousin named Michael Myers. SPOOKY!

Marybeth, Lynn and I use to put on talent shows for Maw-maw. We would practice and practice, then go stand and sing in front of her in the living room. The song 'Nobody' by 'Sylvia' has stuck in my head, I have no idea why.

Let's sing (*Well your nobody called today, she hung up when I asked her name, I wonder? Does she think she's being clever, CLEVER.......*)

We really thought we were something. Maw-maw loved it, and thought it was highly entertaining. "What do you girls have planned for me next week?" she would always ask. So glad we got to entertain her and not just be a thorn in her ass. Which many times we were. I was her personal little thorn bush at times.

Real time: My aunt Beverly and I were just having a dispute on who sang that song. Of course I had to Google her ass. When I showed her, she reluctantly said, "you're right. I'm so pissed." Thanks Google for ending the dispute. Wait, maybe it wasn't Google, I used Safari. How come no one ever says Safari that shit?

Marybeth, Lynn and I, would also occasionally dress alike. One day we took it just a little too far. We had gone to the local department store, called George's. We all bought kelly green chino pants, blue sweaters and khaki blazers. Oh and we all owned a pair of hushpuppies. You know the suede high-top kind?

Anyway, as we were walking down the street in our new attire, some people yelled out the car window at us. "Look at Twiddle Dumb, Twiddle Dumber and Twiddle Dumbest." after pitching them the finger we stopped dead in our tracks, took a look at each other and realized how stupid we must have looked. It hurt our feelings so bad. We thought we were cool, but to our surprise, we weren't. It was stupid! Really, really stupid. Maybe not as stupid as some of

45

today's kids while snorting smarty's or with their pants hanging half off their ass. That's stupider.

I don't recall getting into much trouble, the first couple of years I was at my maw-maws. I was a decently good kid, I guess you would say. Except for the night Julie and I chose to slip whiskey into the seventh and eight grade sleep over at the school gym. Now that was a different story. Hum! Maybe that's why I quit hanging with Julie. Nah!

My maw-maw would never call me out right away on anything. She was calm, cool and collected like that. She liked waiting for the perfect moment. So one morning as I was getting up from breakfast and heading off to school. I must have been a twelve year old smart ass or something at breakfast. Maybe I had a little diarrhea of the mouth. Because as I was about to walk out the door, she peeked around the corner from the kitchen table. "Go ahead and walk out that door, you little drunk." My mouth dropped. I knew in a instant what she was talking about. But why now? It had been weeks since Julie and I had drank that whiskey, and should have been long forgotton'.

With a shaky, surprised voice "What in the world do you mean Maw-maw? Why would you say that?"

"You know what I'm talking about. Don't play stupid with me."

"NO! No! I don't." I was trying to keep an innocent look on my face without looking guilty. I was sure enough guilty, but I didn't want to be in trouble.

"Don't ever doubt my ability to find shit out." she said.

"I got to go Maw-maw, I'm late for school," as I ran out the door.

Do you know I never heard anything else about it.I felt bad, because I had disappointed her. I didn't drink again for at least two

46

years, or maybe just one. Who is counting? Not me. I already said we won't concern ourselves with timelines.

Somewhere in between, I did try me some cigars. Obviously, it was the thing to try at the time. I couldn't just let an opportunity of a new experience pass me by, now could I? No! I think not. It was easy to buy them at the local store. Back then you didn't need to be eighteen to buy tobacco products. Shewl, I'm starting to feel like I lived in the Ice Ages. Anyway, 'Swisher Sweets,' that was the name.

My cousin had talked me into trying them. My maw-maw caught my cousin and I smoking them, that very same day! The same freaking day! Wow.... She is good.... My curiosity got me caught with my hand in the cookie jar. When she peeked out the back door, we were standing in the corner of the garage just puffing away. They were the nastiest damn things I ever tasted. Tasted like somebody pooped in your mouth. I mean so nasty it tasted just like butt, unwiped butt, after a nasty coffee shit. And no! There is no need in wondering how I would know what that taste like. It's just that I can imagine. I also wonder if that's why Uncle Charlie never lights his and just chews on them. Maybe it's less shitty tasting that way.

Charlie and his unlit cigars.

Maw-maw shouted out. "You kids better put that shit out and hightail your ass into the house, right this very instant."

She didn't come out for us, because she had trouble getting up and down the steps. Guess it wasn't as important as going to Bingo.

"I'm not going in. I'm going home," my cousin said.

I got right in his face. "You better fucking come in!" First time (I think) I ever let that word slip out of my mouth, even though I sometimes have it down pat these days. They say people who cuss have a tendency to be more honest. Maybe not across the board, but nothing is across the board, unless you're at the race track. But, if you're wondering why I said that word then. It's because I was pissed and heard other people use it when they were pissed. He was actually trying to leave when I was about to get my ass whooped. I wasn't going it alone.

"No, I'm not!" He replied.

"You heard what she said. We better jump our butts on in there and face the consequences."

"Nope! Not gonna do it. She is gonna cover us in Pledge and wipe the floor with us."

My face was surely turning red. "You were the one that wanted me to try these nasty things, and I'm not getting my hide tanned by myself. You got it?"

"Fine! Fine! Whatever. I will go in."

So as we started to walk in, she backed away from the door to let me inside. Then she came straight at me. This was new. My first reaction was to run. So I headed around the kitchen table as she pursued me. She couldn't catch me. It was like we were playing a version of musical chairs. But the music didn't stop. Even if it did, it wouldn't have been wise for me to sit down. This went on for a moment as my cousin watched with confusion and was grateful that

49

the anger wasn't directed toward him. Then I felt so bad about her hobbling around and chasing me, that I just halted. The music stopped. We stopped. I was standing there wondering what was really gonna happen. At this point she had never chased me, hit me or punished me. She raised her hand toward my head and it was frightening. So I automatically put my hands over my head and let her smack away. She had these rings on her hand that she could never get off. Her arthritis had caused her knuckles to grow bigger than the rings. Them son-of-a-bitches hurt like hell. I took it like a champ, but it sure did put some bumps on my noggin.

A few days later the same cousin was there visiting again. Maw-maw was mopping the kitchen floor when I'm sure that I said something smart ass to her again. She turned right around, raised the mop and swung it around toward my head. I ducked and it smacked my cuz right in the face. An old dirty mop! Yuk!! I have to say, I found it to be quite amusing. Must have been his karma from the cigar day.

Maw-maw had very unique ways in responding to me and handling the situation. Even though I got a few knocks on the head and a mop swung at me, she never gave me any real whoopins. Most of the time Maw-maw never felt like getting out of her chair when she got mad at me. She had no reason to, when she could throw things at me like, shoes and *Rubik's Cubes.* Keep in mind, she was in her mid seventies. She would just pull off her shoe or grab the nearest object and throw it at me from across the room. It seemed like we were always playing a game of dodge ball, but of course, she always had the ball. She was a good thrower, but I was just as good at dodging. Except, the one time when she landed me right in the knee cap with the *Rubik's Cube.* I thought she had done gone and cracked my knee cap. I was rolling around in the floor with pain and all she had to say was, "serves you right."

Needless to say, I got out of the smart ass phase quick. I think I've hit almost every phase in my life. Life is about making mistakes, right? I hope so, because I've made plenty. But I usually only do it once, the SAME mistake that is. Because after that, it becomes a choice and I don't like making bad choices. I don't feel it becomes a bad choice until it makes you feel bad, guilty, or hurts someone. Then I wouldn't dare do it again, usually, with a few exceptions. Ha, there are always exceptions.

Quick story: *While at Saint Augustine, I was in line at school coming in from recess. I looked back behind me and saw a kid put a big slimy booger in her mouth, I mean a big one, one big enough to fill up a kindergarten class. Well, I had to call her out. "Ewwww, what did you put in your mouth? "Nothing," she said. "Yes you did," I replied. "Na uh," she said. "Yes huh," I said back. Then she smacked the shit plum out of me. I didn't hit her back, but we both got sent to the principal's office right away. We were told to write a note on what happened. I wrote mine, then looked over her shoulder to see what she wrote. She put that I had hit her, which was a complete utter lie. That's when my, 'you are not gonna get me in trouble' attitude kicked in. As I said to her in a threatening voice, "I would advise you to change your statement, if you know what's good for you." I'm sure I was intimidating as hell, but don't throw me under the bus when I don't deserve to be there, because you choose to eat your boogers. So after that, a little editing on her part took place and we rolled on with our day.*

THREE OUR FATHERS .--------

So this one night, I had snuck over to one of my friend's house. I want you to keep in mind this friend lived at least 3 miles away and on the other side of town, through the projects and up a huge hill. It was quite the trot.

I wasn't supposed to leave the house while Maw-maw was playing cards. Not because I was grounded, I was just told to stay home for once. I decided to go against Maw-maw's wishes. Readers, I never said I was perfect. Even though as kids you try to get away with things, you know, test the limits and sometimes there is a little lying involved.

While I was standing in my friend's kitchen, chit chatting away, the phone rang. When my friend answered, it was Maw-maw! She asked my friend if I was there. My friend put her hand over the phone. "She wants to know if you're here."

I looked at her motioning and waving my hands. "No! No! I'm not here."

"She's not here Mrs. Luckett." When she hung up the phone, she said. "Your Grandma is pissed and worried. Said she called the house and you didn't answer, she is heading home to check on you."

I looked at her with worry and fret. "LATER."

As I dashed out the door and out into the dark. I ran down the steep hill, while knocking tree branches out of my way. Then through the projects as people's dogs were starting to bark. Then I ran through town and back up the main street. I was running like a cheetah chasing its prey, yes, that fast. As I was coming up a side street that lead to my street. I looked up, as Maw-maws car went cruising by. "Oh shit!" I put it in even higher gear, maybe speedy Gonzales gear. I don't think I even took the time to breathe, but of course we all know I did. I ran behind some houses, and through some back yards, luckily somehow not stumbling over a thing. Faster and faster I ran. I had to beat her home or she was gonna beat my ass or at least tag me in the head with her rings, or fling something at me. That lady had damn good aim, and this time it could be an iron or something. I wasn't taking any chances and I was getting myself out of this mess.

Up ahead I could see her tail lights as she pulled in the driveway and then into the garage. I darted toward the front yard and onto the porch. If any football scouts would have been watching, they would have signed me up for wide receiver. I stood there at the door scrambling to get the key from around my neck as I heard the garage door closing. My hands were sweaty and shaky and I was desperately trying to get the key in. I finally got it and as I entered the front door, I could hear her entering the back door. I darted into the TV room, knocked the phone off the hook, (on purpose mind you) jumped on the couch and hit the TV button. I was panting like a Husky in hundred degree heat, I was bout' to pass out. As I listened to her hobble through the kitchen, I was still trying to get my wind about me. She came toward the room and opened the door. "Missy! You're here! I was worried to death. Why haven't you been answering the phone?"

I looked up with a puzzled look, fake puzzled look that is. "What do you mean?"

"I've been trying to call you all night from my friends house."

"Well, I don't know. I haven't heard it ring." I looked over at the phone and pointed at it. "Look! It's off the hook." I jumped up and put it back on.

Maw-maw just sighed. "Well you had me worried sick, and I had to leave the card game early."

53

"I'm sorry that it worried you, Maw-maw."

"I'm going to put on my nightgown and go to bed. You sleeping in there on the floor tonight?"

"No! Not tonight."

"Fine! Whatever you wanna do." as she closed the door behind her.

"Good night Maw-maw, I love you, hope *Johnny Carson* has somebody good on tonight."

When my heart rate returned to a steady pace, I felt parched. I jumped up ran into the kitchen and drank two glasses of water. Then I had to pee really really bad. So as I headed into the bathroom and turned on the light, low and behold, there stood Maw-maw taking a piss over the toilet. Yes! I said over the toilet, legs on both sides, nightgown lifted. It took me back for a minute, I had never seen this stance before. She just looked at me nonchalantly. "Do you have a problem with the way I pee?"

"No! No! Of course not, do what's easiest for you."

That was the end of that night. I was just glad I had pulled off getting back to the house in time. I really pulled it off and maybe she did too. Wink, Wink. But it was about the only thing I got over on her, she was one slick woman, but I can't believe she wasn't slick enough to figure out the phone line would have been busy, instead of ringing through if it was on the hook. But anyway, I did tell about the lie in confession. I thought God might get mad for me doing that to her. Plus, Maw-maw made me go at least once a month. It was always pretty much the same thing. I would say, forgive me Father for I have sinned. I talked back to my elders and I told a lie. He would reply, say ten *Hail Marys* and five *Our Fathers.* Then I would step out of the booth, kneel in a pew, say my penance, make the Holy

Cross and leave. Then would repeat it again the next month, like clock work.

Short story: My aunt Darlene said when she took her son Joey to confession for the first time, he came out confused. She asked him why the puzzled look? He looked up at her and said, the priest told me to say three Our Fathers, and I only know one.

I don't care who you are, that story is adorable, but on to a new subject. How about cheating? This is a quick story of the first time. It was about homework, second time was a little more serious, but we will get to that later. Hate to already admit to that, you might just get the wrong idea.

So one night, I just didn't feel like doing my homework. So I asked this girl named Dawn, the one in the basketball picture, if I could copy her homework. I wasn't smart enough at the time to not right down all the exact answers, guess I was missing a nugget that day.

So a day or two had passed when our teacher called us in after school. Keep in mind, Dawn ended up being Valedictorian of our high school class. So who's smarter? That's a easy answer, huh?

Our teacher asked, "I know one of you cheated. Who was it?"

I may not be the sharpest tool in the shed, but I knew... she knew... the obvious answer. Dawn wasn't gonna tell on me, and I didn't want us both in trouble. So I rolled my eyes. "Duh! Big red fire truck. It was me."

The teacher pointed at the door. "Dawn, you can leave the room."

So she sat me down and stared me straight in the face. "I have to do something for you cheating, we're gonna have to figure this out.

What kind of punishment would fit the crime?" She didn't seem to want to punish me too harshly.

I glance up, "I know, I understand, maybe something like missing recess."

"Well, I guess maybe, you're gonna have to sit out this weekend's basketball game."

My heart sunk into my belly. "Miss a game?"

"Yes, miss a game. You can still suit up, but you can't play. I will tell your coach."

I leaned back in my desk and pouted. "Miss a game?"

"Yes Missy. Miss a game."

"Please don't tell my dad!" I begged.

"I won't, it's just between you, the coach, and I."

Now keep in mind, Dad came to every game. He was a die hard fan. What was I gonna do? I got it! I'm sick, I will be sick. Look out Father Ernie, looks like I will be confessing this next week. Damn, miss a game, what is she thinking.

So when it came game night, I just sat there on the bench, holding my breath. I really needed to look ill. I hadn't practiced my method prior to the game. It was like acting, it was hard as hell to sit there and hold your breath through a whole game. Believe me, acting sick is a very hard thing to pull off, unless you have *Munchhausen Syndrome.* They are pros and even got a disease named after them. I'm just not that good.

After the game was over, my dad looked frustrated as he walked over to me. "Why didn't the coach play you?"

I was still trying to make myself look pale, "I'm sick Dad, that's why she didn't play me."

He looked a little closer and touched my forehead. "You do seem a little pale."

"Yep, I'm just not feeling good."

That was the only time in my life, I played that sick, I mean really, really sick. Of course I faked the occasional tummy ache to get out of going to school. But it was still hard to pretend. An actress I will never be, although I did pull off an award winning move with Maw-maw and the phone incident. Don't be judging, I'm almost positive all you readers have played sick before too. I'm sure of it. Maybe not for the same reason, but yes you have. Come on! Admit it.

Quick confession: Sorry Teacher, Miss Blank Blank.. I tee peed your house when I was a kid. You know, when you put toilet paper all over someone's yard. It's not because I didn't respect you, or you would have gotten the eggs instead. I was just young and stupid and peer pressure is rough. Plus, this one was not my idea for once, even though you made me miss a game.

I remember the first time I got really mad at my dad. It was gonna be my last and final game at Saint Augustine. Just before that, I had entered a free throw contest and I made it to the finals. Well...the finals fell on the same day. I wanted so bad to play my last game with my friends, but my dad made me go to the free throw contest instead, I was sad and I was mad. You know, that teary eye kind of anger.

I didn't win that day, because I was gonna prove a point that my heart just wasn't in it. I threw up brick after brick, even with all the bricks I thought I was throwing, I still came in second. I guess I'm not that good at throwing away the game, even if I try to give it a valid effort. Just not in my blood to pass up any kind of opportunity.

Thought of the day: *It's not cool to be a fool.*

Now, we all know I was in Catholic school, and had to do the usual things like confirmation. What is that you ask? I'm still not sure, something to do with confirming you want to be a Catholic. My daughter Summer had to do the same thing. Yes, I know, it's religion, a Catholic thing, and since I'm Catholic, I should know the whole idea of it, but I don't. What I do know, is that I will never again sit in the pew ten rows back on the right side of church. Because I got to be witness to the grossest sneeze of the century, maybe even a lifetime. One day while at church, one of my classmates sneezed a softball size snot ball into her hand. She looked at it, then wiped it under the pew. I almost puked in my mouth a bit, I swear at the time, it was one of the grossest things I had ever seen, even more so than the girl eating the booger, which was disturbing enough.

Kevin, Maw-maw, me and Jeff at confirmation. Me wearing a
skirt, is about all I remember.

Let's mention a little about Jeff. Kevin, we will get to you later.
Jeff is the one who use to make fun of Marybeth and hit girls with
balls. Later in life he hit them with other balls. He and I basically
grew up together after I moved to Maw-maws. As you can see, Jeff
is a cutie and I believe most of you would agree. All the girls in high
school thought he was eye candy. I mean he use to drive them wild.
All the girls would go watch him play football and basketball. They
would even show up at softball games just waiting for him to take
off his shirt at the end of the game, while all nasty and sweaty. As he
walked off the field past his entourage, he would just smile and
wink. He could pick from any of them that he wanted. He dated at
least four of my really good friends, from grade school thru high

school. He was very charming and a player and boy did he know how to play. I would warn them that he was a heartbreaker and a rebel, but of course none of them listened and they just kept falling in love. I watched heartbreak after heartbreak.

Me and Jeff and Travis in a box.

OBSESSION

When I received my first real camera, my obsession began. Ha-ha, bet you thought I was obsessed with love. Oh! I was, we will get to it. But picture taking, was my obsession and passion. I would have taken picture on top of picture if I could have, and that I pretty much did, as you all know. Picture processing was expensive and I had to save every dime I had to buy film and to get them developed. Maybe that's why I wasn't eating lunch. I took pictures all the time, and yes, besides taking pictures, I thought I fell in love with a boy while I was in the seventh grade. My first heart throb. I was obsessed with him too. Pictures and him, him and pictures, pictures, pictures, pictures. Boy did I love pictures.

I collected and took all kinds of pictures of him, this boy, whom I thought I was in love. I would write his name over and over in a notebook. I would look up new sophisticated words in the dictionary that meant really good things, so that when I would write him a note, I would seem really intelligent. I remember the word '*scrumptious*' being the first big word I used. I was so impressed with myself, when I told him how scrumptious he looked.

He use to call me every night and we would talk on the phone for hours. It always sucked when someone else needed to use the phone, and I'm not talking about when someone in the house had to, I'm talking about the neighbor. Remember when we had to share the phone line? You had to wait for Miss Gilly to finish her conversation with Myrtle. It was a party line, but not much of a party..

I would play him music on my little record player that I received for Christmas several years before. Our song was, *"Your kiss is on my list"* by *Hall and Oates,*

61

Travis and I

We would also talk about the prank calls we would make. That was our entertainment back in the day. We thought it was so funny and no one had caller ID to catch us. My favorite prank was when I would call someone and ask if their refrigerator was running. When they would reply "yes!" I would get so tickled when I got to reply, "you better go catch it." Cheesy? Yes! Rude? Yes! Inconvenienced people? Yes! But we were kids, come on! At least we weren't making booty calls.

A couple friends of mine always got to throw parties. What kind of parties? Ha! Make out parties. Yep! You read that right. When the parents would come down the basement steps, we would all scatter like bird seeds in the wind. The goal at these parties was to have someone to make out with, if not, you were the lonely girl in the corner or the guy making an ass of himself. I somehow always rounded me up a make out partner. Kissing was a nice activity back then, but our parents didn't think so, or may I say my maw-maw.

Short moment in time: Right before junior high school started, Mom sat me down and asked me if I wanted a brother or a sister. I said that would be awesome. Then the situation was never spoken of again, but that question would eventually lead to two very big events in my life...

So I finally graduated from eighth grade, don't remember much about it or the summer. Then I moved on up to the Junior High School. It was also right down the road from my house and located on the same street. Marybeth, Lynn and I walked to school everyday, no matter what the weather. It only had three grades, 7th , 8th and 9th. It wasn't till years later when they moved the ninth graders to the High School. So at that time we had to attend the Junior High for one year, because Saint Augustine only went up to the eight. We had just previously been the oldest when we graduated from Saint Augustine, now we were the oldest again. It was awesome getting to be the oldest two years in a row without having to fail a grade. What's cooler than being a kid? Being the oldest kid of course.

That year went by so fast that I hardly remember a thing about it. Except that I almost got a severe ass paddling by one of my teachers. Luckily for me, my classmates helped me argue my point and got me completely out of that sticky situation. It really was a terrifying moment. Why? Because when she took people out into the hallway for a paddling, you could hear the echo through the whole damn school. I mean it would echo in the halls so loud it would make you leave your seat every time you heard the bang! Shewl, that was close. Thanks classmates. We would be very convincing lawyers, I hope at least one of you have become one. I would have been a lawyer too, if I wasn't afraid to speak in front of captivated audiences.

While attending Junior High I started to play basketball for the high school, the *Lady Knights*. Even though I wasn't going to school there yet, we were still considered part of the high school team. After school, I had to ride the bus there for practice, no walking involved, thank God, because there was plenty of running once there.

UPDATE: *Lady Nights just won the 2013 State Championship. Woot! Woot! Not such an update now, just because it took me three years to write this and hopefully soon, I will finish this. I also want to thank Nicole for help editing this one. Especially when she drew me little pictures that made me laugh. Like on this paragraph. I had written champion ship. So she drew a little boat with champion wrote on it and said this is a champion ship. Hope you all got it.*

As we all already know, Maw-maw would always go to play bingo. She was old, but she was always in motion, kinda like myself, or lets say, I'm like her. If she didn't do that, she would play cards at her friends several times a week. She would host one of those card games every other week. I loved helping her prepare and I always loved snack time, except when she would break out those damn fake orange slice candies and the marshmallow peanuts, how gross. Every now and then they would let me play a hand or two. I loved playing nickel, dime with the old ladies, they were some damn good people. I'm not much of a card player or gambler these days, I may give it a shot once or twice a year. If I depended on winning something free or by gambling, I would be living in a box. Lets just say, I'm not lucky in that way, although I feel as if I'm lucky in my unluckiness, but we've already discussed that.

I started to dabble around with drinking at this young age, while maw-maw was away doing her thing. I had just recently met a new friend Betina, she was a couple years older. She would hook up Marybeth, Lynn and I, with some pure grain on the weekends. We would mix it up in a gallon jug with fruit and punch. It was something we call hooch or jungle juice. Not sure that pure grain was a wise choice. You could light that shit up like a blow torch and watch it burn.

After we would consume a bit of the tasty beverage that we had concocted. Betina, would take us riding through the roads of the county. One time we decided we would go to the golf course, not sure why. It was raining that night and we were all drunker than hoot owls. When we pulled up, we all jumped out, then I took out running toward the green. "Lets see if we can get a hole in one." I slid across the putting green like I was sliding into home plate. I believe Lynn followed suit, but not Marybeth and Betina. Remember me telling you Marybeth was a girly girl.. she is, but.. oh... She enjoyed trouble and excitement, she just couldn't bring herself to do it. She was a watcher, not a doer. She was too chicken shit to break the rules. But she sure liked to watch when someone else did. Thank God no one ever found out it was us, because we did tear up the green a bit. Oh shit! What is the statute of limitations on that?

We always would get our buzz on while sipping our juice while riding around with the cassette player blaring and wind in our hair. She would drive us way out to Birch Springs. That's where all the underage drinkers would go. It was the next town over. Well it really wasn't a town, but it wasn't Lebanon. It was a cool creek that ran down beside of 'Makers Mark Distillery' You could smell the

66

whiskey for miles. This is bourbon country you know. Why we weren't drinking bourbon, I haven't the slightest clue. Later in life, it would become my drink of choice. Back then we were just experimenting with all alcohols, cheap and strong.

When we would reach our destination and stop the car, we would all jump out and crank up the music even louder, especially if "*John Cougar's I ain't even done with the night*" was playing. The song kinda fit the bill, because we never really were done with the night. We would be out by the creek, drinking our hooch and singing our asses off. I looked over toward the car one night and Marybeth was on the hood of the car dancing like '*Tawny Kitain' did* in that video of *White Snake*. Must admit, we always got a little out of hand. I guess you would say I was a little wild. Some parents would say, BUCK WILD!!!!

My hair had grown out pretty long, since the bowl cut, the curls, the little boy dew, the pigmy look and so on. At least I never fell victim to the mullet. Somebody needs to put an end to that shit, it really should be illegal. So this one particular day at school we were having some kind of dress up thing-a-ma-jig. I decided to go all out. I wanted my friend (my childhood cigarette smoking friend from Raywick) to cut all my hair off. Not just a trim, I mean short, short. I handed her the scissors, as she hesitated. "Missy! I can't believe you're letting me do this. You are one brave soul."

"Cut it! Just cut it! I want to go as '*Olivia Newton John*' from the video '*Lets get physical.*' It will grow back out."

Clip! Clip! Clip! Piles and piles of my hair laid there on her floor. Moral to story? Not sure. Spontaneity?

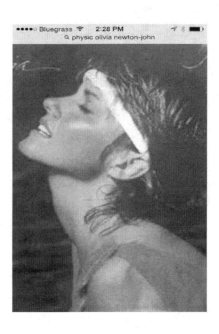

BTW. --- Video killed the radio star?

We didn't really have a graduation party from this school. But I did get invited to go with Lynn and her parents (Jackie and Sandra Owen) to Florida that summer. Lynn's parents both taught at the high school and treated me like one of their own. I wasn't use to family vacations, and it was quite the treat. This was the first time I remember seeing the ocean, it was amazing. Although I wasn't very excited about getting in it. Why you ask? Cause I don't like the taste of salt water or that the fact sharks might like the taste of me, salted. Oh! How about another reason? Maybe a near death experience when I was on vacation with Mom and Dad.

I decided to enter the water anyway, against my better judgment. We were all standing in a triangle. That would be, Marybeth, Lynn and I. All of a sudden a big sting ray swam right between the three of us. We all looked at each other horrified and desperately scrambled to the shore. It's eery not knowing what lurks beneath you. May I insert Summers stingray story in here? No! Lets wait. How about my shark story now? Nope, lets wait.

So what do you do at the beach if you don't like getting in the water or you don't like sunbathing either. My mom was a sun whore, but that's not one of the traits I got from her. I like to play in the sun, not lay in it. I have never found baking in the sun to be very relaxing.

My daughter Summer loves laying out and she stays brown as a biscuit, but then again she was born brown as a biscuit. I was probably more the color of a white turnip. Thanks Dad.

But anyway, I don't like sitting still. I'm a little more active than that. So tanning just isn't my thing. I can't even sit long enough for the hair dresser to dry my hair. When she is done with the clippers, I jump from my chair and say. "That's good."

Then I pay the lady and head out the door with it wet. As she yells, "someday I'm gonna finish the job."

I yell back, "yeah right! Good luck with that!"

So while Lynn and Marybeth had to get their tan on, all day, every day. I spent most of my time at the pool, diving off the diving board and listening to music. '*When Doves Cry.*' by the artist *Prince* was a huge hit on the radio at that time. They played it over and over again. I think of that vacation every time I hear that song.

Note: Songs are a very good memory jerker. They can yank you right back to a moment in time, reminding you of the people and things of your past. It's almost as good as pictures. I said almost. Sometimes songs take you to a place and time you don't want to remember. So you just got to rewrite that shit in your head and make a new memory to it.

Moment in time: *I forgot that I did go on a vacation once with my dad's sister's family. The only thing I knew about trips up to this point, was the ones my mom would take. I don't recall much of it, except 5 of us kids in the back seat, fighting over where we were sitting, I ended up getting the floor board. I know, that has nothing to do with anything, guess I didn't want you feeling sorry for me thinking I never got to vacation. Let's move along.*

Another moment in time*: Summers stingray story. Lets go ahead and get to it. She was only around eight and a teeny tiny squirt. I took her to Discovery Cove down in Florida to swim with the dolphins. It was a fabulous experience, but you could also swim with the stingrays if you wanted to. We thought this would be a grand idea. It was this big manmade shore with an island in the middle. So we get in and start to swim across. As I look back, a stingray five times the size of Summer swims right over her head, pushing her down under the water. She went into complete shock and panic, as I tried to reach out and grab her toward me. She came up grasping for air as she scrambled to get to the rocky island. When she finally got to the edge, she franticly climbed across the rocks. I couldn't even grab ahold her she was moving so fast. She was shaking terribly, when she finally got to the rock she felt safe on. I sat there on the rock with her, as I noticed she had torn her knees to pieces. We sat there for a minute, while she caught her breath. As we started to observe the situation, we realized, our only way off the island was to swim back across. Boy! Was this kid not happy, nor has she ever forgiven me.*

SUMMER!!!!!

Real time: While sitting here at the computer during my January hibernation. Yes! It's the month I like to hibernate, watch tv and eat lots of snacks and put on a little extra poundage. I still find it hard to stay focused on the past stories when new ones are raining on me. Because around here you can't escape the drama. I think my ass is about to turn into a hermit. I want to write about them so I can keep them fresh in my head. But I have to get there, up to date that is. How long will the road be? I have no idea. All I know is that I spent all day taking notes off my phone, writing them down in categories. Only to put them in categories on my computer. Then I try to come back to them later and to write about stories in those notes. So if you're wondering why it took me so long to finish this book. Just know that's a lot of time just moving around notes. Even when I go back to them, most of the time I don't remember what half the notes mean. Do you know what I mean? Do you feel my pain?

----ITS GONNA HURT-----

Woot! Woot! Headed on to the big high school for the big tenth grade. Our county had four grade schools, one Catholic school, two middles and one high school. The High School is where we all came together as one. We all had friends heading in, but when we all got to high school everyone started joining different little clicks. Now I'm not a big click fan, but, I somehow found myself in the middle of several groups that I really liked, didn't want to pick just one.

They were sort of friends to each other, but didn't really hang with each other on the weekends. Only if there was a mutual warehouse or field party. There would always be two or three different carloads of girls that would go out on the weekend. I would hang with one on Friday and the other on Saturday and some on Sunday. I would invite one group over for homemade Chimichangas one day, then take the other group up to my uncle Charlie's cabin to camp. Then head out with some others to do doughnuts or go climbing up Mt Gilboa. (It was an old fire tower lookout.) Some of us went tracking through the creeks, crossed swinging bridges, and climbed the water tower. Even slid into the rivers a time or two. The list goes on and on. Wow! There is a lot to do in the country. Not sure which of these adventures will make it into this story, but some of them are sure to come.

Marybeth and Julie

Meanwhile, when the shit hit the fan between these clicks. I was always caught right dab in the middle. One group would think I was talking about the other, when in fact I never did. You know, girl drama. Somebody has to be talking about somebody. Even though I refused to ever take a side, unless I was one hundred percent sure who was in the wrong. We have all seen enough teen movies to know what this is all about. Haven't we *Mean Girls.* But luckily I chose my friends wisely while growing up. You gals are the best, each and every one of you, you are some damn good people. I have to say, Summer chooses her friends rather well also. And no! We don't choose on social status, but character, character is the key. We were all taking DramaMINE. Because we pride ourselves on being real. Check out the *Dramamine* girl on *You Tube.* Hilarious! Wish I would have thought of it first. Please watch it.

Even though I was at the high school now, I still never had to take the bus. I got lucky and Lynn's dad would pick me up every morning for school. After I made friends with people who had their license, I would get picked up by them. It was way cooler than a bus or riding with Lynn's dad. Even though he was cool, it's just a teenager thing, you know what I'm saying. So, one day this guy named Steve, came to pick me up. As we backed out of the drive, he kept going! He never put his car in drive. Like literally, he just kept it in reverse and drove backwards all the way there. It was more exciting than riding the Beast at Kings Island. Although at that time in my life, I didn't even know what the Beast was. With him, I didn't need a roller coaster anyway.

I was an (out in the open) wild child, to be honest about it. What you see is what you get. I never try to keep my own secrets, don't much care for secrets. From where I'm setting and what I've seen, they always just crawl back up your ass and bite you. So I choose not

74

to always be looking over my shoulder. But you can tell me yours and no one will ever know. That's your business and I will keep it that way. So those of you that are nervous about my writings, I will never tell your secrets. You're safe, I promise. I will only tell things that are already known to others. Scouts honor. Unless you piss me off. Naw! Just kidding! Still wouldn't, or would I?

Quote: *"The greatest advantage of speaking the truth is that you don't have to remember what you said." - Anonymous -*

So we all know I liked to drink, but I also had responsibilities and took them seriously. I've always tried to balance work and play, that's what life is about. I played basketball and I was a starter. My coach was a lesbian who had coached ball there at the school for quite some time. She totally love-hated me. Why you ask? Because, basketball players weren't suppose to be the partiers, they're suppose to walk the line. But I performed to the highest of my ability, so there wasn't much she could say. Even when she caught me at the smoking tree. Yes! We had those back then and were allowed to smoke at school. All she could do was walk by and shake her head. I would just wave. I was pushing my luck I guess, or maybe, just maybe, I was honing my skills and confidence of living uniquely and non conformity. Some would say, by my own rules. Yes, I know I was smoking. Bad! Bad! But that's not my point. We will get to my point.

So, one drunken night at the VFW. A place where we youngsters use to party. I created a little chaos, unintentionally of course. This party place sat on top of a hill that was covered in slate rock. We had all been inside drinking and dancing the whole night. When it came time to leave, I stumbled out the door and a mishap happened. What kind of mishap? Well hold on let me get there. We were headed to the car and I decided to take the hill route for some reason. The one with all the slate rock, I said screw the steps I guess. Somehow I ended up rolling down it like a Tumbleweed blowing in the desert, except not quite as smooth. I didn't fall as gracefully as I usually do. So when I hit the bottom, I was just laying there in my drunken stupor. Wondering! What the hell just happened? Everyone kept screaming at me. "Get up! Come on clumsy."

"I can't..."

"What do you mean you can't?" Someone yelled.

"I can't, there is a rock on my hand. Get it off, it hurts."

They all rushed over. While all staring down at me, someone said, "Can you move?"

"Just get this rock off my f***** hand, please!"

I heard someone else say, "how come she can't move just because she has a rock on her hand?"

Then someone else replied, "maybe because she has a big rock on her hand."

When they removed the rock, blood was spraying everywhere. I had split the top of my hand wide open and completely down to the bone. Tendons and veins were hanging out everywhere. When I would move my fingers, I could see them jump back and fourth, unattached. It almost had me tranquilized just looking at it. My friends were scrambling to grab me up from the ground. They said they were gonna rush me to the hospital. I was rebelling. "No! Stop it! I don't wanna go to the hospital."

When they got me to my feet, I slung my arm around. Blood flew across one of my friends face. I don't think she knew it at the time, but she looked like she herself had been slaughtered and just came off the butcher block.

76

"You're gonna bleed to death if we don't take you," someone screamed.

"Well…. I'm gonna get murdered anyway if you take me there drunk. I will be fine." As I stumbled and slung my arm around again. Blood went flying right across the same girls face once more. I actually started to laugh for a moment. This time she felt the blood spatter her in the face.

As she wiped the blood from her face, she was getting aggravated and stomping her feet. "Damn it Missy! We are taking you, like it or not."

"No!" I yelled again with authority.

"We'll see about that stubborn ass." She said, sternly.

So they yelled for one of our friends. He was a big… friend. He was a football…. player. He came over and put me straight up in a bear hug. There was no escaping his grasp, although I tried with all my might to wiggle out of his arms. "Let me go damn it!" I was kicking and screaming.

He squeezed even tighter, then he stuck me in the car. He held me down, while someone else drove. I was determined not to go, but a 99 pound injured drunk girl, definitely wasn't gonna wiggle her way out of this one.

They finally got me to the hospital and took my ass into the emergency room. Somehow they had gotten' ahold of both my parents! I mean both of them showed up! Obviously you don't need cell phones in a small town like this. Shit gets out fast. So my friends left me there to be eatin alive. Well! That's what I thought at the time.

Mom and I sat there waiting to be taken back to a room. Dad just stood there with concern. I'm sure he was worried about my basketball career. Mom and I just watched with amazement as the tendons jumped back and forth in my hand. It was quite entertaining and painful at the same time. She looked at me with a serious look. "I think you might bleed to death Missy." Then started to laugh.

"Mom! Stop it!"

The nurse showed up just in time before this conversation went south. Mom likes to tease you with her extreme point of view. So after I got to the room, they told me our little rinky dink hospital wasn't gonna be able to put Humpty Dumpty back together again. Why? Because they said I needed major surgery. So they decided to send me to Louisville. They just wrapped up my hand and sent me on my way. I looked at Mom and Dad. "Who's taking me?"

My dad said. "I will."

Mom started getting wiggly all up in her pants. "Well! I'm riding with ya'll. You ain't leaving me behind."

Oh shit! How is this gonna go down. I had never been in the same car with them since I was about four. Actually don't ever remember being in the same car with them at all. This was gonna be one hell of an experience. I was more worried about that, than my hand.

We all jumped in the front seat of Daddy's car, me in the middle of course. We pulled out and headed to Louisville. Mom kept saying. "They're gonna stick that needle in you and it's gonna.... hurt...."

"Shut up Marceline!" My dad said.

"It's gonna be this…. long," as she held her arms out as far as they would go.

"Mom stop it!"

"Baby, I'm just telling you. It's gonna... hurt."

"Mom!" I was beginning to sound whiny and somewhat desperate.

My dad was getting really mad at her. His sense of humor is somewhat different. I knew Mom was just messing with me, but tonight just wasn't the night for that. He was getting madder than an old wet hen as my grandma would say. Mom continued to bug me in her own loving way as her and Dad bickered all the way there. It ended up being the longest ride ever, up to that point anyway.

But what seemed even longer was laying on a gurney out in a cold hallway at the hospital, all alone. They left me there for hours, as doctors and nurses were shuffling people in and out. I was thinking this is some bullshit. They had made Mom and Dad wait in the waiting room. All I could think about, was what kind of punishment they were cooking up for me. Especially after I arrived, the nurses asked me if I had been drinking. I said no of course, but as I looked over my shoulder, my mom was lip mouthing to them, A Lot, she has been drinking a lot. So I knew, they knew.

It was up in the wee hours of the morning when the hospital workers finally got around to me. They lifted up my arm and gave me shot after shot in my arm pit. They were trying to numb me, but the anesthesia wasn't working. After about seven shots, my arm finally went numb.

When they rolled me in the surgery room the lights were bright as hell and the room felt like an ice box. They had music playing for some reason and I remember the song, *Every Breath You Take* playing. It literally burned into my head, because I felt like I was being watched by everyone. I know they played more songs because the surgery took all night.

When it was all done, they rolled me back out and into a room that Mom and Dad was waiting in. I had a huge cast on my arm. Mom and I went into the bathroom so I could get dressed. When I went to put my arm through my shirt, I fell over and smacked into

79

the wall. I had no control over it, none what so ever. That was one heavy ass arm. Mom and I was cracking up, as I pushed myself from the wall. We heard Dad say, "what the hell is so funny?" Then Mom replied, "nothing Buddy, you wouldn't find it funny."

Not sure why I needed a cast, because I didn't break anything. They had sewn all my tendons and stuff back together. This mishap had lead me to my fourth scar. These days it is a pretty hideous sight. You can see the scar tissue inside my hand. When I move my fingers, little balls of scar tissue move back and fourth. The surgeon said it would all dissolve, but he was wrong, wrong, wrong.

I have to keep in mind, these scars only show where I've been, not where I'm going. As crazy as some of these stories are, I kinda like where I've been, for the most part. Now that it's all said and done. I mean, I could do without the hospital visits, but still.

But where I was going at that moment, was nowhere. It put my basketball playing career to a halt. Over the next few months I had to go to therapy and get my cast changed several times. They would put some different contraption on me every time. The last one was a cast with something on the top of it that resembled a crane with rubber bands tied to it, so I could practice using my fingers. It definitely was an eye catcher. I didn't start to feel helpless, until I realized I couldn't fix my own hair. That was a job for Marybeth in the mornings before school. When she didn't show up in time, I got to go to school with bedhead. I was hoping it would start a new trend.

Paula and me!

During the time of no play is when partying with my friends started to escalate. I mean what else was there to do in this town, that didn't require alcohol. We had no theaters or bowling alleys. Nothing! Absolutely nothing! So we drank and did all the stuff I talked about earlier. In our little minds it took alcohol to create those events. We were discovering ourselves and sowing our oats. It was a rite of passage. I feel it only becomes a problem when you choose

81

not to grow out of it. Also, we need to be very thankful that we survived it all, and I am.

Sorry that I keep talking about when the drinking began. Guess it escalated at different times and now I'm just giving you excuses. You can call bullshit if you want! I would. But just know that I was still determined and made it back into basketball right before the season was over. I became one of the leading assist players in the school. Sorry if it sounds like I'm tooting my horn, but I just want you to know my determination won.

------REALLY MOM.... AND DAD...

Okay once again readers, I don't know if this story happened before the hand injury or afterwards. I'm thinking afterwards, but not one hundred percent sure. I just don't want someone calling me out on it later.

So one day out of the blue, my mom pulled up in her old Pinto. I was very surprised to see her. She told me to hop in the car. "Hold on I got to tell Maw-maw." Which I did and we headed off to Campbellsville. When we got there, she pulled over, put the brake on and looked over at me. "You're about to turn sixteen. Do you wanna try to drive?"

"Here? In this car? It's a stick and it's still illegal for me to drive. I don't have my license Mom!"

"So! Do you wanna drive or not?" as she got out of the drivers seat and walked over to my door, sticking her head in the window. "You gonna drive or not?"

"Okay, Mom! If you insist, I will give it a whirl. Hope there aren't any Po-po's nearby."

She wasn't too worried about breaking the law, so why should I be? I put it into gear and headed on my way. I screeched, stopped, died and blew smoke as our bodies went back and fourth with the car. It looked like we were jamming to *Motley Crew* or something. I was so nervous and excited at the same time, as I putted out onto the main highway. But I soon got the hang of it and was hitting speeds up to forty-five. Guess that was my birthday present and I couldn't complain. I had a big shit eatin grin on my face and I was breaking the law. My first law broke, besides underage drinking. That don't count. Remember, right of passage.

Just a few days later, I was sitting and waiting with excitement at my maw-maws. I was waiting to receive my birth certificate in the mail. I had to have this before I could go get my permit. For my parents had lost my real one, and I had to order a new one.

"It's here! It's here!" I screamed, I was giddy as a little girl at Christmas. It's my 16th birthday tomorrow and I couldn't wait to haul ass up to the DMV to get my permit. Being young and yes maybe non observant. I forgot to even look at the birth certificate to confirm its information. I mean what teenager would and why would I? So here is the deal pickle. It's Groundhogs day. I have birth certificate in hand, and I start walking to the courthouse. I get to the Clerk's office with a big grin on my face as I hand her my paper work. I'm thinking, I'm so ready for this test, I'm gonna freakin' ace it. The lady starts to look over the paper work, and as she is reading it, she gets a weird look on her face. Then giving me a poor pitiful you face, she hands it back to me.

"Honey! Your birthday isn't till tomorrow."

With dismay, I said. "What!!!!!"

"Sweetheart! Your birthday is on the third. Which is tomorrow."

83

As I grab the birth certificate to take a look. I see it, yep... 02-03-1968 it says... for real... I mean for real! As I look at the clerk with serious annoyance, "You mean to tell me my parents only have one kid and they couldn't even remember my birthday. I've been celebrating on the wrong day for 16 years. You got to be kidding me! This is amazing! One kid... really! They couldn't keep one birthday straight. They only have one kid..."   SO 'I' THOUGHT.

I seem to have had my share of car wrecks in my life. People say I'm over my nine lives limit, maybe I've got nine lives times two or maybe three. Maybe God forgot he gave me the first nine, cause I've used those up just in car wrecks.

My daughter thinks she has the same curse when it comes to wrecks. Maybe it's not really a curse at all. Maybe it's the whole adventure of it. Sometimes even some of the worst of stories seem to bring laughter or meaning into my life and others. Some not so much, but definitely all the car wrecks can be made fun of now. Especially since I came out unscathed.

When I was in high school I couldn't even make it through one year without one. Trust me, Summer can't either. She is in college and still crashing into people and objects. I guess *GMC* could have hired either of us as their personal crash test dummies.

Hold on, I'm getting ahead of myself. We will get back to all of Summer's crashes later, even yours Mom and Dad. Back to me wrecking cars. I will never forget the first wreck. Well, I won't really forget any of them. It was the first time I thought my dad was going to kill me, actually kill me. I sat in the emergency room, watching him sway back and forth on the heels of his grey leather boots, that I had given him for Christmas.

His arms were crossed and he had a look on his face that I knew was gonna lead to murder. His lips were pinched tight as Spanxs on a fat lady. He was really trying to control his anger, we were about to end up on *Dateline*. I dreaded to hear what he had to say or what he was gonna do. Up until this point in my life I had never seen him this mad. I prayed I had broken something on my body, if not, he may just do it himself. I wanted to avoid his wrath and get some sympathy, so I started to cry out of desperation, I was like the little boy who cried wolf.

He stuck his finger in my face, and said with authority and anger. "I told you not to be driving."

"But Dad! We just rode over to her boyfriend's house."

"What difference do you think it makes where you went? I told you not to be driving anywhere except to your friend's house. You don't even have a license yet. It's just plain stupid that you were driving with a kid in your car while only having your permit."

"But my friend has her license," I disputed.

"Yes! But her little sister was in there with you and that's not legal. I don't know why you can't get that through your thick skull."

I acted stupid as I huffed and puffed. "It's not?"

"No! Its not! And you know its not. You just took the test, so don't be trying to pull the wool over my eyes. How in the hell did you take down a light pole and total out the car? How fast were you driving?"

"Not very fast."

"Bullshit!"

I wanted to tell him to simmer down. Because I felt as if we about to lock horns. But if I would have said that, or even debated the issue any longer, I for sure would have gotten slapped straight across the face. Even though my dad had only laid his hands on me once, back when I was younger and being a whiny baby. Nothing serious. I was pretty sure I had just given him reason for the second.

"Dad it was raining and it was slippery. We had just left David's and her little sister was struggling to get in the front seat. We were trying to tell her no. I wasn't paying attention to the road. I thank God she didn't make it to the front, because she could have been hurt really bad. I feel really terrible for this."

"Do you know you broke your friend's nose? Do you know that the insurance is gonna go up?" He said, sternly.

"Yep!"

"Really! Is that all you have to say?"

"I don't know what else to say Dad. Sorry!!!"

He was still hot under the collar. Death by Daddy was a scary thought. I was for sure dead. Nope, didn't happen, even though at the time it felt like a near death experience was about to go down. He grounded me, but we didn't let Maw-maw know, because he didn't want to worry her with the wreck. We hid it from her, but I'm sure she eventually knew, she knew everything. We already know she wasn't the type to bring it up, till she felt she needed to. She used her information as leverage, when needed. Wish I had her patience.

But the grounding didn't keep me home! Shit..... I had a field party to go to that weekend. Of course I had to hitch a ride. Low and behold, soon as I arrived at the party, some friends ran up to me and informed me that they had spotted my dad there. He wasn't there to find me, like most parents would be doing. He was there to party himself. He was single and ready to mingle.

I had to leave the party as soon as I got there. My friends slid me right back out as they covered me. Safe... but I did lay low after that. I was pushing my luck maybe just a little too far.

A few days later, my friend and I went to look at the car. It was quite amusing I must say. Since we had survived the ordeal, we could see the humor in what we were looking at. As we approached the car we noticed something that looked like a big set of breast sticking out of the front windshield. Both our heads had pushed out two places in the windshield after slamming into the telephone pole and actually breaking it in half.

When we looked at the windshield from inside the car, we could see big clumps of our hair stuck inside the cracks. We also noticed there was a cigarette stuck in the air conditioner vent. Both hoping that no one else noticed. We were still too young to be smoking. Guess that three packs of smokes that made us deathly ill, didn't deter us from the dangers of smoking.

"WOW!!!! We did a number on that car," I said with amazement.

"We sure did!"

"How is your nose?" As I touched her face.

"Broke! How do you think it is?"

"Broke!" I replied.

"How fast do you think we were going?" She asked.

"Obviously too fast."

"Yep, I guess we had to be, to break that pole in half like that."

"We are lucky, huh?"

"Everything but my nose," she said.

"Broken! Yeah, I know! Sorry."

I forgot to tell you which friend this was. It was my childhood neighbor friend from Raywick, and the one who cut off all my hair. Her house burnt down after I moved to Lebanon. Yes, her house that sat next to Grandma's burnt down too. I don't know what the hell is up with all these fires. Has anyone asked my Mom where she was?

While still just having my permit and after becoming ungrounded. I would head down to the car lot and pick out a car to drive. Dad would ask. "You got a licensed driver with you? There won't be anybody else other than that in the car will it?" Of course the answer would always be yes and no. Then I would pick up all my friends and let them drive, permit or no permit. I had a few friends that couldn't drive worth a shit and it scared the hell out of me. Marybeth was even too chicken shit to try it. All I can say is that she missed out.

Sorry Dad! We were big shit now. Plus, Mom had taught me not to worry about the law, so I didn't. Although I have learned since, you do not mess with the law. Just like the song goes, I fought the law and the law won.

I don't know that you would get away with any of that today, but in the eighties we sure got away with a lot. It was awesome. We would ride around listening to my favorite song at the time '*Missing You*' by '*John Waite.*' I had it recorded because of that silly boy I was obsessed with. He had broken up with me in the eighth grade. But I was over it. I now had a girl crush and had to pretend to still like him. I knew he didn't like me and it was easier that way. Didn't have to explain my singleness to anyone. Why don't you have a boyfriend? Why wont you date him or him or him? I mean I did date some hims, but reluctantly.

All my friends say they can't help but to think of me when they hear that song. I branded it in their heads. When my friends sing it, they sing, Missy you, instead of Missing You. I'm certain it was because I had it recorded it three times in a row. I didn't want to waste my time hitting rewind. Who does that? Me of course. We didn't have the luxury of skip back then, like we do now. It made total sense to me.

Eventually my dad got tired of me driving and asking for his cars off the lot. Why? Because I think I may have dented up another one. Plus, I had my license now and I was always on the move. So he bought me an old Chevy Nova to tear up. It had an eight track player in it and that's when I was introduced to the group, *The Cars.* It came with the car and it's the only eight track I ever owned. I knew every song by heart. It was easy when that's all you had to listen to. I would ride around in it belting out the words to the songs. *You're just what I needed,* or, *you might think I'm crazy hanging round with you.*

This was right around the time I tried pot for the first time. We were out riding on some country roads, higher than the Georgia pines. I was in the back seat with some friends, while some other friends were up front driving. Well, all of them weren't driving, just one and with no shoes. We got pulled over and when the officer walked up to the car, my friend and I couldn't do nothing but laugh. He asked the driver where her shoes were and she said. "Sir! I lost them in the creek." That comment sure didn't help me stop laughing, my friend and I just put our heads on each others shoulders trying to hide our faces, I mean tears were coming out of my eyes. If he had said, step out of the car, I'm pretty sure I would have crawled out. Even if he said, Ma'am your going to jail. I'm still not sure that would have stopped me from laughing. I mean that was some serious killer laughing weed. Why he didn't take us all in, I will never know. Maybe he just thought we were all very, very, happy.

Don't remember what happened to that old grey Nova. Did I wreck it? I don't remember. I just remember driving one of those old long ass, boat floatin, Monte Carlos after that. I definitely wrecked it.

It was New Years Eve and I was in the clear for sure. But nope! I had to take out a car in a parking lot in downtown Lebanon only hours before the ball dropped. Just a fender bender, but a wreck, nonetheless. My fender was attached tightly to the other persons fender, like new lovers in the night. Now that's tight. It took a bit of man power to get it detached. Once it was released, I headed off and celebrated the New Year. Yep! I still celebrated. The way I look at it, if you can't do anything about your situation, you just keep doing what you planned. The deed had been done, so just ride it out and wing it. My cousin Jamie knows all about this Philosophy, but we will have to get back to his wrecks later. I've got plenty of my own to talk about.

Oh! I can't forget the 1968 red convertible Mustang my dad promised me for my sixteenth birthday! I never got it. He sold it right out from under me to Lynn's Dad. Then her dad gave it to her for her sixteenth birthday, which came just a few weeks before mine. But luckily for me, she let me drive it many times. I explained to her it was only fair.

Then there were a few more and then a few more wrecks, but we can't just talk about wrecks. We got to move along. Just know, that I have owned and driven and wrecked a wide variety of cars. Plenty of other people have wrecked while I was tagging along too. For instance, the time I was riding with Lynn. She got us slammed head on, one day while taking her cat to the vet. It wasn't in the Mustang, but some old brown car I think. I seen that shit coming a mile away, but sad to say, she didn't. When she went to pull in, I screamed! "TRUCK!" She froze like piss on a zero degree day. There we sat like sitting ducks halfway across the yellow line. The truck sounded off his horn. A big fat ass gas truck. It slammed right into us head on and dragged us quite a ways down the road. When we came to a stop, Lynn's first concern was. "Oh my God! Where is the cat?" That was that. Yes, the cat lived, it was stuck under the seat.

My aunt Beverly said, she knew there was a deep seeded reason, why she would never ride with me after reading some of these stories.

Skipping on to another subject. 'Skipping school.' I soon learned there were no rules on how many days you could miss. So I took total advantage of that. It was quite easy for me to do, while living with Maw-maw. I could get notes from her and notes from Mom and Dad also. Neither one was none the wiser of what was going on. They would both ask me. "Aren't you missing a lot of school?" I was thinking you don't know the half of it. Like when I would call my cousin Kerry from the pay phone and tell him to call the office and pretend to be my dad. It was just that easy back then.

Several times as I was walking down the vocational hill, to head to another class. I would see my car just staring at me from the parking lot. It was talking to me, Please! Drive me. So I would have to grant its wishes and go to it and drive. I talked a few of my friends into joining me on several occasions. My friend Karen was always game. Just know the following year, they put a stop to all that. They put a limit on how many days you could miss. Not sure if it was because of me, or just time to do it.

Just a note: *My friends and I would sneak to my dads house out in Jesse Town and throw parties when he was away. He said he rode by one night, and there were people sitting on the roof. He never said why he didn't stop. Guess he was just gonna let it ride and let us party on. Or maybe, just maybe, he was taking a lady parking. He would never admit to it if he did. There was a street right down the road called Lovers Lane. I'm sure he ended up there a few times in his life, like everybody else in the county.*

Daddy's grey boots. The backs are rubbed off due to all that
rocking he did at the hospital that night.

Soon I started dating this boy, we will call him Jake. He is the first guy I had sex with, yep! That's what I said. Sex! We all know I've had it, lets not act surprised.

We had been dating for around nine months. He kept asking me to have sex. Then he begged and begged then begged some more. He told me if I did it, he wouldn't ask me again. Not sure if he was expecting it to be bad or if he was just trying to get his way. I ended up getting really drunk one night, and we did it in my maw-maws guest room floor. Was she home? Yes, she was. Taboo? Yes, again! Ignorant? Of course. Luckily she stayed fast asleep. Keep in mind, teenagers don't make the best decisions while under pressure or drunk. I just remember the experience not being so great, definitely no details to reveal, and definitely nothing I was ready to try again any time soon.

A few days later he asked for it again. Guess his experience was a little better than mine, imagine that. I responded with a straight up answer. "Sorry! We are going to have to break up."

Good thing! Soon found out, he had also been in cahoots with another girl from the county over. There became a rivalry between me and that girl. Mainly because I was his last girlfriend and she was jealous and I had to defend my reputation. It wasn't just because that either, but also because of basketball. You know how U of K and U of L are, it was something like that. The closer the team lives to you the bigger the rival. Like you really want to kick their ass every time you play them. I don't mean just win, but leave parts and pieces of them all over the floor. Tear them apart like a dog would a biscuit.

93

Anyway, this bitch had the audacity to show up at one of our local field parties. Now mind you I'm not a fighter, but she didn't belong here with her rootin' tootin' friends. My friend Carla looked over at me with annoyance. "What the hell are those bimbos doing here? And why is that one staring at us? Isn't that the one that has been messing with Jake?"

"Yes it is and those Yoyos aren't gonna be here for long."

I was trying to pick a bone when I yelled. "You bitches just need to go ahead and leave."

Yep! I was being a bitch. It happened from time to time.

Carla was getting agitated from my agitation. "Hey! Hey! Get out of here you little whores."

We were both giving them a warning and maybe a challenge. It must have scared them right away. They ran and jumped in their car, don't guess they were looking for a squabble. Then we ran and jumped in my car. Not sure why. They were obviously leaving. Guess we were looking for a brawl. Anyway, when they pulled out, I decided to follow. What was I thinking? I'm really not sure to this day, except maybe to look like a bad ass in front of my friend. I still don't know why I would do that, because I don't even like people who act like bad asses. We ended up chasing them all the way to town. We literally chased them ten miles up the road. We were really trying to wrangle them up. I don't know what I thought I was gonna do if they stopped. Guess we could have had a dance off or your momma so fat competition. When she got to the red light, she sped right on through. So did I.

Sirens sounded off. Woooowoooowooowooowooo.

Carla starts smacking my arm jumping up and down in her seat. "Oh shit! Missy, Missy! It's the cops! Ooh shit! We are fucked."

I thought it was we, but once again, it was only me. The one who was fucked that is. The one in trouble. He had pulled me over on the main highway. It was just a few short minutes from Maw-maws house and mine of course. If we had been in Carla's car, I may have jumped out and ran since my house was so close. I could have eluded them. No! Not really. That's nothing I would have done.

The officer walked up to my window and pecked on it with his knuckles. The blue lights were lighting up the night. I was sweating with fear and with apprehension, as I rolled it down.

He asked, "Young lady, can you step out of the car?"

I looked at Carla worried stiff. She and I knew I was in some deep shit. When I got out of the car, my eye level only reached his badge. He was standing there tall and stern with his hand on his gun when he asked, "Do you know you just ran that red light?"

"Yes sir! So did that car in front of me."

"I'm not worried about the car in front of you."

"Why not?" as I tried to debate.

"Young lady, have you been drinking?"

Of course the answer was no. Then he asked me to step onto the sidewalk and take ten steps. He said do it from heel to toe. I was on pins and needles as I started walking. Damn if I didn't take eleven steps instead of ten. I tried desperately to stop at ten, but my foot just took one more. Oh lord! That's not good. I clutched my hands and prayed he couldn't count. Was I wasted? Heavens no! Not this time. Was I drinking? Yes! Yes, I was.

My aunt Beverly jokes with me, and says I counted wrong from skipping so much school.

But anyway, he looked over at Carla with suspicion. "Young lady have you been drinking?"

She through her hands up in the air. "No sir!"

95

"Well, you can take this young lady's car home if you want? I'm taking her with me."

I mean Lord sakes, he didn't even test her. He just took her word for it. Why didn't he take my word? Oh! Yeah! The extra step. I watched her drive off. Then he proceeded to put me in his cop car and took me to the cop station, not the jail. Yes, there is a difference.

He walked me in and sat me at a chair. "Young lady! I don't really want to book you. Do you have anyone you can call?"

"Yes, sir," I said with a sigh of relief.

So I tried calling my dad, no answer of course. So the only other person I could think of at the moment was my aunt Libby. She is my dads older sister. I had remembered her number because I use to always call her kids. After I got her on the phone, I told her the officer said she could pick me up, if she didn't mind. The cop told me if he saw me back out in the streets, he wouldn't be so nice the next time. But as soon as I got to Libby's, Carla came and picked me up.

"Come on Carla, lets go back to the party."

My aunt Libby seemed a little concerned, when she said. "Didn't that cop tell you to stay in?"

"Why yes he did, but Carla and I got to go back to the party. We didn't even tell people we were leaving."

When we arrived I spotted my dad talking to some of his friends. I walked up to him with my head slightly down. "Guess what?"

Then he responded with sarcasm. "What? Did you wreck another car?"

I kinda rolled my eyes. "No!"

"Well, what then?"

"Um... I just kinda got locked up. Not really, more like pulled over and taken to the station. Then released and here I am." As I threw up my arms, like ta-da.

Here is the weird thing. I don't know anymore of the story or recall him saying much more about it either. I'm sure maybe he just slipped into deep depression and wondered what he had done when he had sex in the back seat of that Chevy. Maybe I'm just blocking this shit out. Did he punish me or not? I don't remember. Damn! Have I repressed the memories? I'm thinking he was just a cool Dad and understood that teenagers do stupid things from time to time. Maybe I'm just like Aunt Frankie, no memory at all.

Hum... and another thing I'm wondering. How the hell did I get hold of Carla? We didn't have cell phones back then, but somehow, we always managed to find each other.

My daughter Summer is still amazed on how we knew where to find everyone and where the party was. Summer is like. "Mom! How is that possible? I couldn't survive without my phone or be able to get in touch with anyone." She truly believes that. It's a constant, where is my phone? Have you seen my phone? Where's the charger? Have you seen either of them? My phone, my phone, my phone. Boy, I miss the days not having to worry about that. Life before cell phones was so peaceful. I hate that phones have become an extension of ourselves. They might as well go ahead and surgically insert them in our wrist as a child. Seriously, why not?

Short story:

One time. When a younger friend of mine pulled up to someone's house to pick them up. She called his cell phone. Then looked at me and said. "Missy! He isn't answering the phone. What do we do?"

I replied in complete laughter and disbelief. "You go to the door and knock, or you could just blow your horn."

"Missy, you are such a smart ass."

"Well, Nicole. I'm just saying."

THE OTHER WOMAN

Just a few months after almost going to jail. I got back with Jake. No sex, of course. We were hanging out kinda like a couple, but not really, not in my mind anyway. We had fun together as long as he wasn't asking for sex. I still wanted to be dating someone cause everyone else was at the time. Pretty lame reason, huh? Come to find out, he was getting it on with a mutual friend now. Guess he had to get it somewhere.

She and I both ended up at Hardee's parking lot one night. That's where we all used to meet up in our cars to hang out. Then we would just drive up and down the streets. We would drive to TG&Y parking lot then back to Hardee's parking lot. Over and over again. Honking and waving and looking for guys. I remember always stashing a five dollar bill in my back pocket for safe keeps. Because what I was looking for at the end of the night was a big juicy bacon cheeseburger combo. Thought I was gonna say something else didn't ya? But anyway, we would all be starving at the end of the night. I would pull out my big five dollar bill like I was doing a magic trick. I always seemed to be the only one smart enough to stash the cash. Maybe that's when I became so concerned with feeding the hungry. Because I always had to share and give them a bite.

But anyway, there he was. Jake!!! Standing there at the end of a car hanging with his friends. When he looked around and saw the two of us standing in the same group, he hopped into his car like a gutless pig and left. The girl came straight up to me and got in my face and was fussing. She was screaming throwing out a string of profanities and blah blah blah. Keep in mind, I'm not easily intimidated. "Is that really your opinion woman."

"Yes it is!"

"Listen here. He is the one duping us both. I'm not lying to you and you're not lying to me, but he is trying to lie to both of us. Not trying, but has been."

She stopped and shrugged her head. "Hum.... your right. What are we gonna do about it?"

"I tell you what we're gonna do. We are going to go confront him."

"Where do you think he went?"

"I'm sure he headed home, cause he is a yellow belly like that."

So we hopped into my car and drove to his house. There sat his car, so we knew he was home. His room was located in the basement of his mom's house. So we entered through the basement door without knocking and barged straight toward the bedroom. When we flipped on the light, he was already in bed. When he saw the two of us standing there, his eyes got huge. Then I think I smelt a little stank in the air.

"Shit your pants did ya?" I said.

"What are you two doing here?" With a crack in his voice.

"We're here because you're gonna make a choice." I demanded.

"A choice?" as he stalled and stuttered with confusion.

"Yes! A choice!" as she and I nodded in agreement.

Then she put her hands on her hip and demanded an answer herself. "It's her or me? Which is it Jake?"

Then he stared into the air looking for an answer, as he laid there still wrapped in his blankey. "Well... If I have to choose, I guess it would be Missy."

So we turned off the light and walked out the door.

"That's, that!" She said.

"Guess so." I replied.

Don't know why he chose me at the moment. I wasn't given him any. Wasn't much of a win, but whatever. I think he was getting it on with her by the end of the week. You get what you accept and we didn't last long. Plus I wasn't gonna give it up again anyway. No way! No day!

Just a note: I've never understood why women blame the other woman. It's the partner's responsibility to be loyal, period. Unless it's your best friend, then that's a whole nother ballgame. We should handle things like in the movie 'The Other Woman.' We should join forces and burn his ass, not literally burn him, but you know.

Mom and Gate

Somewhere during all of this, my mom had moved in with Gate. You know, Paw-Paw Gate. They were living in Lebanon in a house they rented behind some apartment complex. So one day when I was driving home after school and jamming to some *Whitney Houston's* 'How will I know' and bopping around in the car, I decided I would give her a visit and tell her about my week. I pulled around the apartment and back into the drive. As I was pulling in I was somewhat confused. Not somewhat, totally. I noticed there was no house. What! No house?

It was burnt to the ground. UHH…. Where is Mom? She didn't even call me and tell me. What the hell? Where is she? Is she okay? As I yanked my car into reverse and wheeled it out of the drive. I was worried and confused. I knew she was Okay, because I would have been told if she wasn't. I never found her that day.

She is a very hard woman to keep up with sometimes. One minute you see her, the next you don't. She has a tendency to disappear like Houdini sometimes. You can even ask Gate. Sorry to dread that up Gate, but the truth is the truth. He use to have to hunt her down every now and then, back when they were married. Every time I hear that *Brooks and Dunn* song, I think of them. Here's a few words to the song.

"I lost her trail on a Friday night, she was gone before I got home. She'd been getting restless, in the big house all alone. I've been up and down these city streets for three nights in a row, and Lord its hard to find that girl, when she get's the urge to go. It's kinda like a lost and found in a border town, asking about a diamond ring. They just look at you, like you lost your mind, say they haven't seen a thing.. But I know she's been here lately, I can still smell her perfume, she gets crazy…. on a full moon."

Sorry Mom! You did like to disappear back in the day. Don't be mad when I tell them about a few more of your disappearing acts soon. You know. Like at the Casino. Abracadabra! Poof.

Mom at Bickett's Bar getting ready for a disappearing act.

Junior prom 1985

Jeff and me and no that's not Jake.

I don't have a crazy story about my junior prom, only that I went. But I do have a story about Jeff and I at the Club 68. There was a girl there and her name was Cow Patty. She was a rough, tough and one mean ass mother fucker. She ended up shooting this feller I know. Rumor has it, she cut off someone's fingers too. Anyway, I knew she wasn't one to be messed with. I was in front watching the band and swinging my hair to some AC/DC. BTW, I hate AC/DC, but that's what they played at the club, So I made the best of it. Back then I was more of a Madonna, Bryan Adams, kind of girl. I liked sappy music too. Yep, Yep, sappy music. My friends would always ask, what the hell are you listening to. Especially when I played the theme song to *Saint Elmo's Fire*. It wasn't nothing but instrumental, now that's sappy.

But anyway, she looked at me and tried to hand me a joint. I leaned back. "No thanks."

She got up in my face. "Why in the hell not?"

She looked as if she was gonna kick my ass if I didn't. Like I was offending her or something. It wasn't peer pressure, not even bullying. It was worse. That bitch was not to be messed with. I wasn't trying to get high, but I wasn't trying to die or lose a finger either. So I took the damn thing from her hands and took a big hit. Like a *Cheech and Chong* hit, just to impress her. It was a bad idea. Everyone's voices started to slice the air. They were coming in from every direction. Houston, come in Houston. It sounded like Charlie Browns teacher times a hundred. I was kinda getting freaked out. When she turned and looked the other way, I darted toward the door. I made it outside, I desperately needed air. I hid beside the building till I came back down to earth.

I started walking toward the parking lot, when I spotted Jeff sitting on the back of a car, with a beer and a cigarette. He was laughing. "What are you laughing at?" I said.

He pointed toward my car. When I turned and looked it was sitting on top of railroad ties. "Did you do that?" I asked.

He chuckled and said. "Nope!" Then he started to laugh again.

I looked around and threw up my hands. "Well! Who the hell did? Charlie Brown and his fucking buddies?"

He replied with a laugh. "Don't know, could have been." At this point I realized he might have been as messed up as me. I was trying to figure out the situation and who in the hell did this, but really I was too stoned to care. It became quite a funny situation. But the thought was still there. Would it move? So I jumped in to see and when I hit the gas the wheels just spun in the air. As Jeff started to sing. "The wheels on the bus go round and round." Obviously Jeff already knew it wasn't going anywhere, because he never removed himself from the hood of the car.

"Just forget it" I said. When I got out and walked back over toward him, his singing turned into a puke fest. It looked like something from the *Exorcist,* as a stream of beer vomit went flying past me. "Wow! What the hell was that?"

I thought that was the end of him, just like my car. But nope! He just smiled, wiped his face and took another drink. Way to suck it up Jeff. As far as how we got home, I do not have the answer. My mind went blankety-blank.

Quick update: It is fall, 2013. Jeff is now older and his cuteness has turned into rugged good looks. He looks a lot like *Joe Manganiello* that plays a Werewolf in the show *True Blood.* He is now married to a wonderful person named Tina and has decided to leave all the other hearts alone. I feel he is gonna need to be remembered. Because, here thirty years later, I just found out he has cancer. Don't really know what kind, but definitely not looking good. They gave him the strongest chemo available. In most cases it makes you sick for days, but not Jeff. Each day when they were done with his treatment, he got up and walked right out the door and hopped on his motorcycle and continued working and living his life. He as always been a rebel and has never felt that he had to prove himself to anyone.

It's killing me how things just keep changing through this story. Plus, I never anticipated on having to tell many stories on the Luckett clan, especially not this way. They have always been my lucky side.

He may be the first grandchild on my dad's side to pass away, due to this horrific disease. It sucks for the whole family, especially his mom, to have to watch him suffer the way that she does.

Although Jeff was a little heartbreaker, he is still loved by anyone who crosses his path. Maybe that's why he was able to break so many hearts. You just couldn't help but love him.

I will keep you posted on my very dear cousin Jeff. The one whom I grew up with, drank with, prayed with, got into trouble with and graduated with.

At the end of the school year, most of us Juniors attended the Senior Graduation party. It was in a field of course. Like many other nights in this county, many that I haven't even spoken of. Guess we will have to flash back to them later. This party was one wild, crazy and eventful night. I got too drunk to remember much of it. Except for the part about two girls getting into it and one girl trying to cut the other girls hair off. Then I woke up and it was the summer of 85.

I've just decided to skip over this summer and my senior year of high school for the moment. Only because there might be too much shit to tell. So le'ts skip, skip, skip to my Lou my darling, way, way into the future. I'm gonna pull a Marty McFly.

But wait! Before we head out of this segment, I do wanna tell you a quick story of Mom. It was at one of my senior basketball games.

It was the end of basketball season and it was my last basketball game ever. We were in the regional finals, biggest game of the year. My mom had finally made it to a game. My Dad was still in prison, so of course he wasn't there. We were playing a damn good team and our rivals whom we had just defeated the night before were in the stands. One of them being the girl I chased out of town. P.S. I'm a bad ass. Not.

The first half went exceptionally well. We kept up point for point and the score was tied at the half. When we started the second half we just couldn't keep up. We had lost our steam and momentum and couldn't rustle up an ounce more of energy. I was running down the floor, when my pony tail holder fell out. My hair was flying back and fourth everywhere. All of a sudden, I heard people in the stands, yelling TECHNICAL... TECHNICAL.... I thought, What? I looked up in the stands and our rival team was standing up doing the big T sign, Screaming, T! T! T! So I turned around to look, and low and behold to my surprise! My mom was chasing me down the court with a pony tail holder. Do what! I stopped dead in my tracks. I thought that she had done lost her mind. "What are you doing?" as I threw my hands up in the air. "Get off the court! There is a game going on."

"Honey I just wanted to give you this, your hair was flying everywhere." as she was dangling the pony tail holder up in the air.

As my voice rose I said. "Oh my God Mom! Are you serious? You can't be out here!"

The other team was still doing the big 'T' sign, and screaming at the top of their lungs. Everyone else was laughing, even the referees. I mean they couldn't do anything, but laugh. I'm talking some laugh out loud, hold your stomach and maybe slap your knee a time or two.

Mom was so embarrassed that she darted over behind the coach's chair and hid. Laying as low and still as a mouse with a hawk hovering above. There was no technical given of course. That shit was just to entertaining and no one had to pay an extra cent too see it.

The whistle blew and the game went on. I was so exhausted just trying to keep up with the other team. I decided this was a good time to foul out, this shit is a wrap. Plus, a standing ovation would be nice for my last SENIOR GAME. Which I got, and one of the biggest high school embarrassments ever! Thanks Mom!

REAL TIME: I *ran into Pam, a high school friend and teammate the other day at Kroger. I asked her if she remembered us getting into trouble at the L.I.T, back when we stayed at the hotel with the basketball team. We were laughing as I was trying to tell her, that we were staying in the bottom room of the hotel, and people could see in our windows. Drunk people were coming out of the bar located at the hotel and glancing toward our room. So I had a bright idea on how to mess with them. I said that we should all get under the covers and make it look like a bunch of people were having sex!*

110

It worked and people were stopping at the window staring and she said, "oh! That's when someone threw a brick through someone's car window." as I started to laugh, "yes and the night we snuck past our chaperones and ended up locked in a long hallway that ran under the hotel." As Pam jumps in with an obvious case of A.D.D. "You remember when we both drove the car home from practice, like both of us in the drivers seat, that was crazy shit." Thing is, I didn't remember. It's crazy how I remembered one thing and she remembered another. I'm just glad other peoples memory is as bad as mine. So as I was leaving, I asked her, can I use your name in the book, she replied, you better, or I won't know you are talking about me.

The 1985-86 Marion County girls' basketball team is as follows: kneeling, from left, Carrie Gribbins, Missy Luckett, Joan Gardner, Paula Drury, Shannon Overstreet, Mindy Ballard, and Shelly Chasteen. Back row, from left, head coach Beverly Roby, assistant coach Glen Spalding, Aretha Porter, Keirnan, Missy Thompson, Theresa Sandusky, Gayle B assistant coach Freddie Leathers. [Photo by Todd Spaldi

First row, second person, me.

111

How about a blonde joke: *Why was the blonde fired from the M&M factory? For throwing out the W's.*

Life is about choices, some we regret, some we are proud of.. We are what we choose to be. -Gram Brown-

BUILD IT AND.........HAY...

Guess what? The future is here. It's what will become the beginning of my field of dreams. It's about to turn the year 2000. It was the year that we were suppose to loose all technology and the world was gonna crash and come to an end, oh my!

Despite assurances from Bill Clintons advisors that everything was gonna be fine, people still started hoarding food and batteries preparing for the worst. People like Grandma! You know? The prankster and witty one from Raywick, Mrs. Coletta Bickett. She was afraid.

Many people were in fear that computers wouldn't update when it hit midnight. So people started digging holes and stashing their cash, because they were afraid it would put us in a tail spin back to the cavemen days. I'm pretty sure cash would have no value at this point. How on earth would we survive?

I myself wasn't concerned. People and family have tried to scare me with that kind of shit ever since I can remember. Although this incident had nothing to do with the end of the world, just computer crashing, but to most people it meant the same thing. I remember as a child lying in Grandma's floor playing with a pencil or bread tie or something, and everyone was talking about how the world was gonna end. Blah! blah! blah! I remember thinking even back then, wouldn't it just be best for all of us to go together. I don't have to miss you, you don't have to miss me, HELLO! Everybody wins. If it's gonna end, it's gonna end. Not much we can do about it. Except be kind to our Mother Earth and hope she will be kind in return. Even though Mother Nature can be a mean and unforgiving mother fucker sometimes, she can also be just as gracious and I thank her for that. She is a bit bipolar, don't cha think? She needs some meds badly, but I love her all the same.. As you might already know, the end didn't happen. So people! Quit predicting the end. It will end when it ends! No one needs to be marking that date on their calendar. Unless we spot a bomb or asteroid heading straight at us, but then it's to late to mark the date.

I wish Mom and Dad would have named me after mother natures counter part, the weather. That way when someone tells me what to do. I can say my name is Weather. I do what I want, when I want. Just like when I opened my Cafe in September of 2000. I did what I wanted without consent from anyone, except the inspectors. Hold on there, wait a minute, hold up. Let's go back just a hair. I got way ahead of myself. I have to fill you in on this part first, before we talk about my field of dreams.

I had previously graduated nursing school. Yes! I graduated, but no license. Why no license? Because I knew..... I didn't want to be a nurse. So I didn't bother to go take the test or even attend the graduation. I hightailed it out of there as soon as I got my final grade. Bye-bye adios. Why? Because the ailing people would stay embedded in my brain when I came home from the hospitals. I just couldn't take it. Maybe I'm a pussy. But really, I just couldn't take it. Especially when it came to sick kids. Not that I didn't want to help, it was just too depressing for me. I would tell you some stories, but like I said, it's just too depressing.

Oh! Wait a minute! I have a story and it's not depressing, maybe embarrassing. So, I was in a hospital room doing my clinical work, and the teacher was standing there watching me. My project for the day was to give a man a catheter. We had already been taught the sterile technique and I knew what it was. I still started to sweat, because I had to touch the man part. So anyway, I reached down and picked up his pecker. It was like a shriveled pickle at the bottom of the barrel that no one wanted to touch. But yes, I had to touch it, I was touching an adult penis. As I was coming toward it with the tube, it fell out of my hand and smacked right back down on the sheets, and no it wasn't the tube. I started to sweat even more, thinking; do I pick it up or walk away and start all over? Yes, it was still attached and no I didn't break it off, it was to flimsy to break. It was a very unhappy limp lacking muscle. It was just lying there like a wet noodle. I was in a panic, and of course and made the wrong choice. I picked it back up and stuck the tube right on in. I knew in an instance I had totally screwed up, because the teacher looked at me with the stink eye and waved me toward the door. When we stepped outside, she started to scold me. "Missy, do you know what you just did?"

"Yes ma'am I do. I broke sterile technique." Then I started to argue my point. "His penis was just so soft and in the flaccid stage, that it slid right out of my hand."

She chuckled under her breath. "Well things happen, now don't they."

I could tell she wasn't happy, but she was still laughing on the inside. I'm pretty sure the man survived.

Side note: Keep in mind, It's not how high your IQ is to make it in life, it's your choices. God only knows, mine isn't the highest, mid grade at most. Luckily most of us get a chance to make another choice next time around.

Mom and I

So instead of becoming a nurse, I diddle daddled in several different things. I became a D J and a bartender at my family's local nightclub, which was called Bickett's. It was the second location because of course the first one burnt down. I've got plenty of stories on that place, I mean buchoos, but I doubt I will find the time to tell you in this edition. It would be a book within itself. Actually most of these stories would, if I gave more detail. I'm just not much on detail

I guess. I run through stories like toilet paper in a house full of diarrhea.

Everything I went to college for, ten years worth may I add, I ended up not doing. Everything else, I self-taught myself. First I watched *Bob Villa* to help me learn how to remodel my house. Then I started watching *Emeril Live,* to learn more about food. The self teaching thing worked very well for me and I was wondering why I had spent so much time in college. Since Summer was only around the age four, I had to watch the kiddy shows too, and it was a struggle, I didn't even watch them as a kid myself. *Beauty and the Beast* was the first Disney movie she watched, and to my knowledge the first Disney movie I ever watched. I have to say, out of all those shows I had to tirelessly set through, *Fraggle Rock* was one of my favorites. I'm wondering what drugs that writer was on.

I even had to teach myself to write this series. We all know that I dropped out of English time and time again when the teacher mentioned term paper, so why now? Why write a book? Guess I get bored, or guess I wanna tell you stories. Mainly because I miss my pictures and want to document my life, before I get to senile to remember. Remember folks, my pictures were my retirement plan. It could be that I'm trying to be a Jack-of-all-trades. I have mastered the grill, but sometimes when you have mastered something, it becomes mundane and tiresome. Although I still get excited when I get perfect grill marks on a steak and have to take a picture and share it on Facebook. Summer, these days is stuck on Snap Chat. Oh! It's so annoying. Every time we go and eat she has to Snap Chat it and then states. "If you don't Snap Chat it, it didn't happen." I can only reply with rolling eyes, "whatever Summer! It disappears in six seconds. I hope you saved it to your pictures."

Summer in New Orleans

119

Anyway! Back to how it all started, back when I decided to open a small place to cook, in the back of my family's nightclub.

First reason: They kept getting in trouble with the law because they were letting people under 21 in and they weren't serving any food.

Second: I had nothing else I wanted to do, career wise. So I offered my services to help them out.

We ripped the back storage room out and I renovated it with my own money, so I could cook for the bar customers. How did I have money? I was still washing cars at my dad's car lot, so I made an investment.

Once I started cooking, it wasn't long before the word got out that I had the best steak in town. Not sure why I started cooking steaks, but that's what I chose. But a lot of people wouldn't come to the night club to eat. It wasn't the best setting in the world for that, especially after a Friday night when the whole place smelt like alcohol and puke. It was definitely a party place. Plus, I only had room for four tables.

After about a year, Mick, my partner got involved helping out a bit. What I loved most about that relationship is there was NOT a reacher or a settler. We were equal parts. But that's a whole nother' story too. I'm trying my best to stay away from 'by the way' that reminds me moments. It just happens sometimes and I'm trying really, really hard to stay focused on the direction I plan to take you. So back to Bickett's and the back room.

I was only open on the weekends. Mick was the only person that helped out and she already had her own job in Louisville. Other than her lending the occasional hand, I did the serving, waiting, cooking, cleaning, ring outs and everything else associated with running a

Cafe. Most of it was fun, but trust me there are parts you just don't wanna do, like clean out the grease trap. It's a stinky, slimy mess.

Me working.. LOL

My steak dinner was only ten dollars at the time, It was cheap. I always got at least a five dollar tip, which was cool. It meant I could keep the prices down and keep the customers happy. They were happy and I was happy. It was all good in the hood, I mean in the country.

Since I wasn't paying anyone to work or paying any rent, I was making a decent living. I was helping the fam' dam out by serving food and keeping them out of trouble with the law. It was a win, win, situation at the moment.

My steak is said to be delicious. Some people say it's so good it makes you wanna hit someone. I never really got that comment, but I just tell them the boxing gloves are over there. Who came up with that anyway? The saying: 'this shit is so good, makes me wanna slap your momma.' That ain't very nice. I guess it means when you taste something fabulous, you wanna smack your momma for never fixing it before. Just a thought, hell I don't know.

There was one girl who came back there wanting a snack, she had stumbled back from the club. She insisted on some ice cream. So I got it out and sat it on the counter. I put a big spoon in it so I could dip it out for her. You know, the big, big soup spoons. I went to get a bowl and when I turned around, she was eating it down with the same long ass spoon, as ice cream was dripping out of both sides of her mouth. She had to be stoned out of her mind. Shit like that has to make you wonder.

There was also another girl that would come every weekend and order French fries. Mick and I had the biggest crush on her. We would push each other to get to wait on her. Then we would just gaze at her till her asshole boyfriend would come back there and drag her out by her hair. He was such a dick. We were always concerned about that, but I guess it all worked out. I guess the point to that short story is that it was funny that Mick and I had a crush on the same girl, and we were secure enough to admit it.

THAT THING LOOKS REAL?

Mom, Me, Joe Mack and Kathleen. I chopped the hair off again, just can't seem to make up my mind, short, long, short, long.

Guess I'm gonna get a little off the subject here again, but I wanna run through this story real quick. My aunt Kathleen and Uncle Danny had just started this tradition once a year in October. It was called the Leaf Ride. People would gather their horses, carts and buggies, four wheelers and anything that would travel off road. It was a full days ride up through Raywick's knobs and down through Shit Creek. It is country living at its finest.

So Mick and I decided we would go for the first time. The weather was perfect and the leaves were just beautiful with all the autumn colors. We were riding with Joe Mack and a friend of his in a red jeep. We were following the horses, drinking beer and enjoying the view and the clean air. In case you're wondering where Summer was that day. Joe Mack's mother had her safe and sound at her place, in a basket.

A little over halfway through the ride, we took a break on top of Scotts Ridge (the ridge is where you can look off and see all of Raywick, pretty sure I've mentioned it before) My friend Jeremy was riding this beautiful black horse. He yelled over and told me to jump on. I decided to be adventurous and jump on. Once I pulled myself upon the horse, it immediately took off. Him, I and the saddle went flying off. My head hit the pavement as hard as a calf falling out of a cows behind. I went blank for the first time in my life. They say Mick came running over screaming. "Don't die! Don't die!" She almost pronounced our relationship right in front of everyone. I mean some people knew we were together. We just hadn't announced it to everyone. Remember where I live and what year it was. Put it this way, it was a long cry from where we are on the issue now, even though we still have a long way to go to break the hatred and misunderstanding.

According to resources I laid there knocked out for a bit. As I was coming to, they said I was trying to get up. They were trying to make me stay on the ground and lay still. They thought my neck may have been broken. They said I was arguing and saying I had to go cook breakfast for the nuns down at the bar. At that point they really knew I wasn't right in the head. They wouldn't let me up, and they said, I said. "If I can't get up, at least give me a cigarette." What on earth would make me want a cigarette? Damn nicotine just won't let go for anything.

The ambulance came to get me. I don't recall the incident till I arrived at the hospital. I don't mean I recall the actual incident. I guess that's when I got my wits about me back. You know, after the stars went away and the little birdies quit flying. That's when I realized I was really injured.

My noggin got hit so hard, the side of my head swelled to the size of a softball, no joke. It looked like I had an alien coming out of my head. After they admitted me, they released me just as quickly. Why? Because I didn't have insurance at the time, I was indigent.

125

When they sent me home with Mick, they told her if I started to throw up she could bring me back. So after we got home, the puking began. She called them up right away. They said to just keep an eye on me and let them know if any other changes occur. Of course changes were occurring, but they weren't gonna let me back in. What dicks! Guess I needed me some Obama Care huh? Maybe a cell phone or two.

So anyway, the whole week I had to lay on one side of my body with my head facing down toward the floor. It felt as if I had two heads, well actually I almost did. Watching TV from this angle was a bitch. I couldn't do shit! I was bored out of my mind.

The following Friday was Halloween. I wasn't staying at home, plus I had to open the Cafe. Oh shit! I didn't tell you what the name of it was. It was a terrible name. That's why I steal names and sometimes let other people name things for me. Like my first dog, his name was Trap. Why? Because he stuck his nose in a mouse trap at Dads and he recommended it. Then I named my horse, 'My Horse' kind of funny when you think about it. "So what's your horses name?" People would ask. "My Horse." I would reply. "Yes! I know, but what's it's name?" They would ask once more. "My horse."

But anyway the name of my Cafe was B.L. KETT'S. Do you get it? Didn't think so. No one else did either. People just said lets go to Missy's.

Do you get it yet? B...L...KETT'S. Bickett plus Luckett equals B.L.KETT'S. Okay! Never mind! Let's move along, doesn't matter anymore. That's why I changed it.

So Mick and I dressed up like nerds. Boy! Were we nerds. She had gotten some of those ugly ass teeth you put in your mouth and some other accessories, to make her look hideous. Damn! I wish I

126

had a picture. I went as the guy of course. I had on a flowered shirt, with taped up glasses, greased back hair and bright orange pants with a big dildo stuck in them. My uncle Danny bout shit his pants. He kinda just stared at it and said, "that thing looks real." All I could do was laugh and say, "You know what they say about nerds, big brain, big.........."

So, later that evening I'm standing at the grill cooking in my fabulous attire. Mick came running up behind me as she put her hands on my shoulder. "Missy are you feeling okay?"

"I feel fine! WHY? What's the deal pickle?"

"Well! The back of your head is gushing blood and it's running down your back."

"Oh shit! Is it?"

"Yes!"

I felt the back of my shirt and when I pulled my hand around, it was covered in blood. "Shit! I cant be cooking like this."

So Mick finished up what I had started. Then we closed down the grill and headed home. When we got home and investigated the situation, I had a huge gash in my head. They didn't even see it at the hospital because my head had swollen up so fast that it sealed it. Now that the swelling was going down it busted open and it was just plum nasty. I didn't get stitches, because they probably didn't want to see me again. You know, no insurance, no money, no service. So I just let it heal itself.

Wasn't but about a week later I was watching TV and ran my hands through my hair, when a big blob of hair came out, right in my hand. I was in a panic, it just kept coming out. The next morning, I rushed to the doctor and forced my way in, well I didn't force myself, but I had some pull to get in quickly. He ended up telling me I had a fungus in my head. He said that most likely all my hair was gonna fall out. You talking about going into a major panic, I couldn't look like a pygmy again.

So he prescribed me some three hundred dollar medicine. I was poor at the time and that was just a massive amount for me. I got it, because I had to keep my hair. I was completely tore up about it. Come to find out, it wasn't that at all. It was from where I hit so hard it killed the nerves in that spot. I still have that bald spot today. It's just hidden under my massively thick hair. Now my head is funny shaped too, trust me you don't wanna see me bald. I want that doctor to give me a refund. If I was like some people in this country looking for a free ride, I would sue him for the stress that he caused me or at least the three hundred dollars.

I'm wondering if that blow to my head disturbed my memory. It could be a possibility, at least I have an excuse like everybody else.

FYI: *My brain is like a game of scrabble sometimes.*

Yes, that came out of my head of hair, just a thinning.

MISSY'S OUT OF THE WAY CAFE

Okay! Let's see! Where were we headed? Oh! The Cafe. So people kept talking about my place. Word of mouth went further and further out of town. At some point I got an idea: Build it and they will come. Well, it wasn't really my idea. It was *Kevin Costner. A*nd it was a baseball field, but all the same, but different. I had a vision, a vision no one else could see. Build a Cafe on the farm. The idea of this place was an accidental journey, who would have thunk it

When I started to mention the idea, there were plenty of detractors. I got all kinds of people saying. "Are you out of your mind? Are you crazy? You've done lost it. Your cheese has done slid off your cracker." My dad even said, "That's so out of the way, no one will ever come. No one will drive down this dead end road to eat. You are completely off the beaten path. This road ends at the river and no one is gonna come back here. No one!"

Well..... I have to say, that is how it got its name (Missy's 'Out of the Way' Cafe) from my dad.... My big supporter.... but luckily I chose to ignore his skepticism

"Do not go where the path may lead, go instead where there is no path and leave a trail." -- Ralph Waldo Emerson--

"The purpose of life is to live it, to taste experience to the utmost, to reach out eagerly and without fear for newer and richer experiences." Eleanor Roosevelt

So, my idea was to build it beside my house. Summer will be going to school and she can just get off the bus here, at home, and at my place of business. Yea! Yea! This will really work, was all I could think. Plus, I'm not interested in getting rich. I just like to cook and I only have one need. Put shoes on my baby's feet, and maybe a good education.

So, I decided what the hell! I will go with it.. Against everyone's will... and advice..... My dad finally agreed to deed me two acres of land. He just put his head down and shook it as we signed the papers. But he still thought the idea of it all was ridiculous. Luckily he put a little of his faith in me and let it ride.

When I went to the bank to get the money to actually build it. They asked me to draw up a plan. They wanted to know how I thought this idea would work. I was thinking, it's just gonna work. Why you gotta' ask? Even after drawing up the plans they didn't want to give me any money. I kept explaining the concept and talked to a few people I knew at the bank until they finally agreed to loan me sixty thousand dollars. Now! I don't know if you know how much it cost to start a business from ground up, but this just wasn't gonna cover it. So my scavenger hunt began.

I sold my boat and my car. Gonna give you a quick reason on why I had a boat, besides the fact that they're just flat out fun. Someone was supposed to take me to the lake one day. They didn't show up and it pissed me off. I thought well! This will never happen again. So I called my dad and told him I wanted to go to the auction with him. When he asked why? I said to buy a boat. He thought I had lost my mind then too, but he took me. I got one, and that was the end of that. Gonna bring you some boating adventures sometime during this series, depends on how long I live. Remember we're not guaranteed tomorrow. This could be my final segment, who knows? Just know that we about ended the lives of two different people on those boating adventures. Although they both survived that day. Sad to say, one of them is not with us anymore, do to another tragic event. R.I.P. Joey. Miss your goofy laugh.

Just a thought: Tomorrow never gets here, cause as soon as today is over, today starts. So why wait till tomorrow, when you're always stuck in today.

So I ended up buying a five hundred dollar truck to get me from A to Z. Yep a cheap one. It was rusty with holes in the muffler and everything. It was blue, ugly and quite the noise maker. I used it to go hunting for stuff for the Cafe and to do a little partying in, when I could find the time. I collected everything from barn lumber off other peoples fallen down barns, to chairs and tables at yard sales and anything in between. When the delivery drivers delivered the equipment, I saved the crate wood it came in to cover the barren walls.

I made good use of the credit card offers that came in the mail for extra purchases. I would buy things with the cards that had six months free interest. Then I would pay off that one with another one. It worked for my temporary situation. Never paid a penny interest. But you got to be careful when trying to pull that one off. It's a very tricky game. I know way to many people in debt due to this piece of plastic. I won't even let Summer sign up for one. Summer! Stay away from credit cards! I mean it.

So for the rest of the summer, Mick and I spent a lot of late nights over there, dry walling, painting, anything that needed to be done. We weren't afraid to get our hands dirty. We even built the bar that runs completely across the Cafe. We didn't have many tools to work with, we were girls. So to get the laminate bar top to stick, we used our butts as rollers and it worked rather well. It's still holding

132

today after fourteen years. Umm, fifteen now, Um 16 now. Lol, it takes awhile to write a book and with my family adding story after story, it's real hard to focus on the task at hand.

Our second proud piece of work was this old door we found with a mirror in it. We turned it into a wine glass rack that hangs over part of the bar. We would just sit and look at it, while drinking a glass of wine. We thought we had done something really special, and actually, we did. It's awesome to be able to admire your accomplishments sometimes, and the hard work you did to get there.

Oh sorry! The building! It was built by a friend. It cost around thirty thousand just to frame up a tin building. When he built it, I made damn sure he built it high enough for a barn, just in case Daddy was right. Then he would have somewhere to put his hay or tractor, whatever he feels fit. I also got the plumber to put shower drains in the bathrooms. Just in case I needed to rent it as an apartment. I didn't do all this cause I doubted my hair-brained idea. I did it, because it's always smart to have a backup plan. A contingency plan, always...... The way I was looking at it, I wasn't planning on leaving an empty building on my property while owing money to the bank. Especially when only about one percent of businesses succeed. Although I may have been a little scared, doesn't everything great start out a little scary?

Quick thought: I love how everybody has a different point of view on things like that. Example: A friend was here one night and I was gonna make something with eggs. So while at the Cafe I grabbed an extra egg just to be safe. You know, like if I drop one, crack one wrong, whatever the circumstance, I would be covered. But they looked at it like I was setting myself up for failure, that was really their point of view. While on the other hand, I was looking at it

133

like a back up plan, covering my ass. Which is it? I don't know if that
makes me the optimist or her. I would guess maybe her, since her
faith in egg breaking was more confident than mine. OH! I got it, I'm
a realist, knowing things happen. So maybe it's not always best to be
an optimist in every case.

So ...our goal was to make a cake, oops wrong story. Our goal was to make this building inviting. Because white plastic insulation just wasn't gonna cut it. Summer, who was only around seven at the time even helped paint the place. She painted rug rats on the walls, which still remain, can't find it in me to paint over them, even though the wall needs it. She painted little people on the bathroom doors and helped me paint a city scene on the wall. Trust me, she is quite the artist, even at that age. Her painting is on the cover of my first book and this one. Hopefully all the future ones too. I can't wait to bring her more into the story, I just got to get there.

Mick and I had found an old painted canvas at a yard sale. We gathered left over paint from people's homes. Then late at night we would paint the Cafe. We were over there late every night that summer. One night I believe I went a little cray-cray. The paint cans were sitting there open, just staring at me. I picked up one of the cans and just started slinging it all over the canvas. Then I picked up the next one, and the next one and the next one, until they were empty. I was highly frustrated, but somehow I ended up putting that frustration to good use. I had made a beautiful painting by accident. I call that canvass, '**Moment of Insanity**' and it was one of the first things I hung up.

The second thing was a huge James Dean poster that Gate had given to me from the post office where he works. I opened with what little I had. It has taken me up to this date, the day I'm writing, to fill it up. I still have room for donations. Anybody? Anyone?

Put it this way, when I first opened, I didn't have much of anything. Just the bare necessities. I was just a small tater' and a poor one at that point, amongst a field of giants. One of my waitresses use to get excited every time I bought a new trash can. I only started with two and it's a pretty big place. She thought she had to walk too far to throw something away, and she was right. Bottom line, I didn't have the money to be buying anything extra at the moment. But when I did, oh was she excited. Now I have ten.

Quote: "Luxury is not a necessity to me, but beautiful and good things are." Anais Nin

Summers first and last day of work. LOL.

My regulars followed me from my first venture and became loyal patrons. They helped spread the word, even though most people around hear only spread the word of the Lord. I never advertised, I don't believe in it. I paid this place off the second year I was open. My gamble became fruitful. How? For starters, we had a packed house from day one. Secondly, I never went anywhere to spend money and I saved every dime and handed it to the bank. Thirdly I did all the chores myself. Manager, cook, book keeper, cleaner, and so on. Not braggin, just sayin'

I had a waitress who was about twenty years younger than me. She was obviously feeling a little down on her status at the moment when she said to me. "Missy you have more than I do." I replied, "No shit! I'm twenty years older than you. Plus I'm not out partying and spending every dime I have. My ass is up on this hot grill every weekend." Then she replied, "You don't have to be." Of course my smart ass came out and said. "No shit Sherlock! I want to, because I want to pay this place off. I hate! I mean I absolutely hate to pay interest and it takes dedication to do that my friend."

Quote: *"Do what you have to do until you can do what you want to do." -Oprah-*

It wasn't long after that the banks started to call. Oh boy did they call. Not for the reason you may assume. They were asking me if I wanted to borrow more money. Hell... No... I would say. Why would I want money from you? I've got money now. Weren't you suppose to be here for me when I needed it? You know back when I was smaller than a piss ant baby. No I take that back, smaller than a piss ant babies nuts.

People like to compare my place to *Lynn's Paradise Cafe* in Louisville, only for it decor, doo-dads and trinkets. It's like a big mobile for kids and adults alike. It is a beautiful, yet funky and eclectic place that sets here in the middle of Raywick's knobs. People ask me all the time how long it took to put all this stuff on the ceiling and my answer is always. Just hung something today.

Over the years I've added many, many things. Not one, yard sale, ever has to go on here, not on my property. Everything goes on the walls or ceiling, I mean everything. From match books to trinkets from places I've been. Left over cool looking bottles, beer signs, Summer's left over toys, party decor and much, much more. I've got every nook and cranny filled. One part is filled with Mardi Gras beads and what a great place to display them. Although I do get odd looks every now and then. We all know what it takes to get those beads. But keep in mind, I didn't get them that way. OK, maybe once. Once isn't bad after going there thirteen different times. Looking forward to telling you about those adventures.

Looks much better in color. LOL!

So over the years my place has really grown. It has been considered organized chaos since day one. Word of mouth has spread for miles and miles, even out of state. It has been stressful and rewarding at the same time.

I get called Idgie from time to time, since opening this place. Guess I have my own little Whistle Stop, with a steroid shot. Although I have yet to cook a man, like Big George did in the movie 'Fried Green Tomatoes,' but… I've thought about it. Then I say naw! If I have to kill a man, I will just bag em and tag em, and take em to Charlie's and let the chickens eat em. When I think of the movie, it makes me sad. Why? Because the Cafe is gone at the end. The movie is only two hours long. That life story was just a speck in time. Soon this place will be just a speck. We are just a speck here on this earth, just a snap of the finger. Our life moves that fast in comparison to that of time. So let's live it up people and don't blink an eye and get your asses down here for a steak to remember.

If you get here at sunset, it offers a beautiful view that people in the city just don't get. (Ha-ha! Just pictured *farmers only dot com*, "city folk just don't.... get it") cheesiest commercial ever, I mean ever. I'm gonna have to put my dad on that site so he can get a date. Not that he can't get a date, he obviously just doesn't want one. He told me once that he used to drive to Louisville on a maybe, and now he wouldn't walk across the street for a definite. He also told my aunt Darlene, if there was a naked woman and a cigarette sitting on that car, he would pick the cig. He also said he told a woman I would rather mow a pretty field of grass, than to go to bed with you right now. Ha-ha! I doubt it Dad, but whatever you say. But he does love his hayfields. So it may be true. He is always plowing, planting, fertilizing, cutting, tetering, raking and bailing. One day he said he was gonna seed something other than, his alfalfa. I was like why? He said. You cant plant alfalfa where alfalfa is. All I could do was laugh. Why was I laughing? Because of how he worded it. Doesn't sound right does it? You can't plant alfalfa, where alfalfa is. Oh well! maybe it just sounds weird to me

Back to the drive out here. You're gonna see shit loads of the '*Virgin Mary*' in bathtubs buried halfway in the ground. Some people say they play a drinking game to them on the way out from Louisville. Every time they spot one, it's bottoms up. It gets you pretty wasted when you have to take a shot every time you pass one. There is just that many. There would be more, but you just can't put a Mary statue, where a Mary statue is. LOL! Did you guys catch that? You also may see a few signs that say. "Prayer is the best way to meet the Lord, but trespassing will get you there faster." But don't be alarmed, we're not like the people in the movie *Deliverance.* Well! I'm not, can't speak for the ones in the hills, but I hope not.

We never give Yankee directions around here. It's more like, turn at the red barn, take a couple curves, when you see the milk farm turn right and head toward the oak tree. Then take a left at the herd of black cows and if you've gone too far, you will be at the river. Just turn around and head back. Take a right at the spotted horse. Forget your GPS and just get your Christopher Columbus on, you'll eventually stumble upon on it. Leave your flag at home, you can't claim it, I was here first. You don't get to just take it because you found it, but you can buy it.

These hills are still full of rednecks, country boys, farmers, hillbillies and the turtle man. You may be thinking, they are all one and the same. Even some people around here might think so too. But nope! Just not true. This is the one and only time I'm gonna come out and say, you are wrong if you think that. Wanna know why? Let me tell you; or define it for you. Country boys are just hard working friendly boys, with white legs and burnt arms, tight jeans and a little muscle from all the farm work. Most women find them quite sexy, even when they chew tobacco, chew tobacco, spit. While… Hillbillies, well… We know who they are. Right Uncle Charlie? And farmers, well… that's my dad driving around the county roads on his tractor. He sure in the hell ain't no red neck or hillbilly, not really sure he is a farmer, maybe more of a cattleman these days. The Turtle Man showed up here once, years ago. My dad said this man was gonna come fetch some turtles out of the pond, by walking on them, and that he did. That was the last I saw of him, till he got his own show. He is one of a kind, not sure if there is a category for that.

141

As far as red necks. Get your broken down lawn mowers, washer and dryers out of your front yard already.

Raywick towing service. Compliments of my Dad.

NASTIEST THING I EVER SAW

REAL TIME:

I want to tell you a short story that Jimmy brought up the other day while at Charlie's book signing in Louisville. Jimmy (which is my uncle who had the lion) and a couple of my friends were sitting out on the front porch, plus some other guy I didn't know dressed in overalls. Somehow this conversation came up. Not sure what started the conversation, but we will start with Jimmy saying: Keep in mind he was talking about being in Raywick, not Louisville.

"Listen! Listen here! I use to go back in the woods, across the river on the right there. You know way up there in the knobs. I got stuck one night. It was so dark, I bottomed out over a hill. These girls with me are in high heels and long dresses. They gotta walk outta there, it's the damnedest mess you ever saw. I liked to have died laughing. All them girls had went to a wedding. I was completely stuck. I usually get out pretty easy. I would get me a blazer and put big monster wheels on it. You know something like that helps you from getting stuck? But I still bottomed out, don't know how I done it. Stuck! Dark! Pouring down raining. Yep! Walked out of there with them heels on. We couldn't see a thing and all you could here was the frogs chirping their opinion. It was something. Tore up about everything I ever owned.

I looked straight at Jimmy. "You just tore up the lawn mower this morning. I seen ya down Grandmas."

"Yep! I still do. Yep! Look at that truck over there. I put new blades on my disc and I forgot to lift it up. I took off and it slammed around and hit my truck. Yep! You know! I tore the lawnmower up over there at my brothers house. You caught me, I do, I tear up everything. Yep! Yep! Not that I want to. Just like Missy's daddy said there. You know Old Buddy? He said If you're not tearing up something, you're not doing nothing. Yep! I tore up stuff of Buddy's and he said don't worry about it, cause I've done, done it a hundred times. Anything you've tore up, I've done, done it. Her daddy is dangerous to work around. It's a wonder he has an arm, finger or anything left on his body. He runs wide... Open, all the time."

I put my arm on Jimmy's shoulder. "I'm expecting to find him up there tackled by a cow one day. Laid out flat as a pancake in the mud."

Jimmy kinda leans down out of his chair and starts to whisper. He does that when he is about to turn the story up a notch. "Hey! Look a here! Buddy will bend down, he'll get in there and cut them

143

there cows nuts out. I will hold their tail up there like that. He'll cut their thing off with a razor blade, then he will stick that damn thing in his mouth."

I lean away. "Ooh! That is gross! I can picture those bloody balls hitting the ground now."

Everybody cringes a bit as Jimmy continues his story. "Not only is it dangerous as hell, that's the nastiest thing ever. Buddy will stick that damn razor blade right back in his mouth, cow ball blood all over it.

We were still grossing out and my friend seemed to be puking in his mouth a bit as Jimmy continued.

"Hey! He does it all the time. Oh… he has always done it.

I ask with disgust. "Really? He sticks it in his mouth? That's foul. No wonder Mom wanted off the farm."

"Yep! Right in his mouth. Cuts them nuts off and sticks it in his mouth right there. I told em, Buddy you nasty ass thing. He said that ain't nothing and said it's all alright. Okay, Buddy I said. But let that calf kick you in your mouth with that razor blade stuck there in your mouth right there like that, then see what happens. He somehow gets by with it. He is sixty-five and he's done it forever."

"He is sixty-eight." I disputed.

Jimmy responds with a more aggressive voice. "What did I say? I said sixty-five! Twenty dollars on it."

"What did you say he was? Sixty-five? Oh shit! You're right. He will be sixty-six in December."

Jimmy slaps his hands on his knee, then leans back all cocky. "There you go, that will be alright. I know how old Joe Keith is, that's how I knew. I will let you slide on the twenty this time. Just remember. I always know what I'm talking about."

144

Then he rolled on with the story like he hadn't missed a beat. "But Buddy there, he's a dandy. Boys, I tell ya. Yep! He would have made a hell of a veterinarian."

Then the overalls guy jumps in the conversation. "The world gets a little stranger every time a man like him dies. They don't make em like him anymore."

Jimmy says with excitement. "He's got two hundred big cows. I've never seen a veterinarian out there. He pulls all his cows, unless it's a major, major thing. Like if one has to be cut open and worked on or something. But other than that he does all the stuff himself though."

"What's pulling a cow?" the guy asked.

"You fool! It's getting a calf out of its momma. You just stick your hands up in there and pull it out. How the hell do you not know what pulling a calf is?

"Well hell! I didn't know, never pulled one. Just cause I got on overalls doesn't mean I'm a farmer."

"Oh well! Whatever! Its messy, especially after the afterbirth is just hanging there."

I laugh, "Next subject please."

Jimmy puts his head down in thought. "Well, lets see here. Buddy use to have a big pig operation when he married my sister. I went out there one time way back before I went to prison. He had hundreds of pig. Hell! Four or five hundred of those Yorkster pigs. They were all running around and we were walking out there through them. He would see two or three dead ones laying there on the ground, he would just pick em up and throw them over the fence. I asked, Buddy, wonder what's wrong with them? Awww, they just die, he said as he started to laugh. A lot of people would say, lets take them to the vet. Yep! Yep! He is a tough old bird, I will tell ya

145

that. He goes over that gate pretty fast when an old cow gets after em. I can't believe he still gets over it. He's gonna get hurt one of these days, you wait and see. If he lives long enough, he is gonna get hurt. You know we slow down when you start to get our age. He thinks he can still get out there with them. He'll see, you just wait. He will get a lesson or two real soon."

I said. "Daddy has made me get out there with him when he is rounding up cows to get their calves. Man! You're not gonna be able to go nowhere near that cow when it has a young calf. He tells me to stand my ground. But I'm just out there doing this shit, waving my hands. I'm like, dad! This ain't working. He yells at me again. Stand your ground. I'm like okay! whatever! How the hell do you stand your ground when the mother cow starts digging in the ground like a bull? I mean it was staring me down like this was gonna be my final hour. Then dad yelled at me again, hold your arms up. That cow put its head down and took a step forward with snot flying out his nose. I said to hell with this. I turned around and took off running. She was on my heels, I swear to God I barely made it over the fence. I literally had cow snot dripping off my ass. It was that close. Scared the hell out of me. But anyway, like I said, I'm expecting to find him up there trampled by a cow one day too. I think he would be happy with that kind of death."

Jimmy nods his head. "He gets right out there with them like it's nothing."

I start to laugh. "I gotta tell you this. We set up there at the Cafe and watch every year when he rounds em up the cows to get the calves off them. It's quite a show when they're chasing him around the barn and knock him off his four wheeler. He thinks he has the upper hand, but they have got a hold of him a time or two. When you try to separate them from their calves, boy they get mad don't they?"

146

Jimmy smacked his knee. "You better believe that."

"Then they chase the trailer all the way out the lane. Then I get to listen to them bellowing and hollering for the next few days, because they're looking for their damn calves. It's not a sound you wanna hear every day."

Jimmy starts in on another story. "Yep he will cut the skin off one calf and put it on another calf. He has twins all the time. So if another Momma's calf dies he will just strap the skin around one of the twins. He will just tie it with some string there. Then he will turn it loose and that old cow will smell her calf and let it suck right on."

I put my head down. "Boy! That sounds nauseating. I shied away from that farming shit quick. I don't like it. I ain't ever farming again. He has got me out in those field a couple times, but that's it, bout lost my life both times. Then he got me in the pig barn and he got me ran over by two huge pregnant sows and their tits. Smacked me right across the face."

"How the hell does something like that happen Missy?" Jimmy said.

"Well! Dad would make me kneel in front of those little chutes they have to go in when they have their babies. You know, to keep them separated from each other. There is a place for the little ones so the sow won't lay on em and kill em. You got to take em and put each sow in chute till they have their pigs. So he was trying to get them in and he said squat down there behind that board while I try to get these two in. I got all nervous and shaky and said, down there behind this board? I'm telling you I was a nervous wreck."

"Aww Miss, You weren't nervous." As Jimmy smacked his knee.

"Whatever Jimmy! He had this big shock thing. You know them electric ones and I just knew he was gonna use it. I'm like daddy

147

don't! Don't you dare! Don't you dare shock them! Don't shock em! Don't shock and…. he shocked em. They plowed me straight down. Sow tits bouncing right over my face."

"How many titties do they have?" Overall guy asked.

"Twelve a piece. That makes twenty-four. Slapped with twenty-four titties."

"You should have liked that." Jimmy said with a large laugh.

"Shut up Jimmy!"

"Well finish the story."

"Keep in mind they're hanging down to here. All the way down on my face. They have milk in them, and there they go right across me as I'm flat on my back covered with the board. Them tits were smacking me right across the face. Slap! Slap! Slap! Twenty-four times. I got up and I mean I was like shaking! I was like, I QUIT! I'm done! It smelt terrible to start with."

"Yeah! Those things are pretty stinky."

"I would go in there and when I came out, oh my God! I smelt horrible. I mean my hair, my clothes, my body, it was just wretched. You don't want a whiff of that shit. Like I said, I rebelled, I quit. God... It was disgusting.

Jimmy smiles real big. "Awww….Buddy! He is something else."

FYI: *One of my dad's greatest passions is farming.*

148

FEAR US NOT

Okay readers, back to the Cafe. People in the olden days use to fear this place. Not my place, but Raywick itself. I never thought I would end back up in Raywick, but here I am. It still has a lot of stigma wrapped around it. I sometimes hesitate to say I'm from here, only because I never know what kind of reaction I'm gonna get or what kind of stories they have heard. It's like a mini Vegas. Only difference is, what happens here doesn't stay here. It usually hits the headlines and if not Charlie publishes it. Whether it be about pot, all the bar fights, the rumored dislikes of African Americans and several murders that have hit the headlines on *Americas Most Wanted*.

Don't forget, we also have Johnny Boone, (AKA) known as, head of the *Cornbread Mafia*. He has been on *Americas Most Wanted*. He is also being hunted down like a wild boar, by the FBI, even though he hasn't killed a soul. He didn't live here, but made plenty of appearances. He would always come in the café and have a salad and coffee. He even showed up to my first Halloween party and kept all the guest high. He also would randomly show up on Grandmas porch. Think he had a crush. Or maybe, just maybe, she was the head honcho, the matriarch.

And of course you know I'm just kidding Grandma. Even though you look like a lady who could run an Empire.

I tell people I'm not a true Raywickian. I know you're thinking how can I not be one? Well I'm not and I have tried to escape on numerous occasions. I guess I am just a plain ole true Raywickett. You get it? Raywick, Bickett, Luckett. Yep! That's what I am, a

Raywickett. Even so, I still can't escape the stereotype. It's just one amongst many. Stereotypes just stick to people, sad to say.

Just the other day when I stopped at a local barber shop in Lebanon to see a friend. I asked the ladies in there why they haven't been down to the Cafe. They responded with, "Oh hell no! We black people. Wheeze ain't coming to Raywick. We will get shot!"

I laughed. "Not at my place, we ain't like that. You're safe."

"You sure about that girl?"

"Of course I am."

Even a lady that I ran into in Louisville the other day, said she use to live in Loretto. She said her mom dared her to ever cross the Raywick line.

Stigma? Yes! Next town over? Yes!

Back in the eighties, if you were lost and not from these parts and happened walked into one the Hatfield or McCoy's bars, you might have found yourself in an uncomfortable position. I hear you would get a stare down like in one of *Clint Eastwood's* western movies, right before a shot-em-up and get asked. "Boy.... You ain't from around these parts, now are ya son? What do you need? Why are you here? What do you want to know?" They were always suspicious. Things they were doing were usually illegal. Mostly like selling pot. If you were an outsider that wasn't invited in, it was best to just stay away. Safest thing for you to do back in those days.

Now days it's a bit different. Over here I have worked hard on breaking down the racial and outsider barrier. We are welcoming to all. From the farmer down the road who pulls up in his farm truck, to the bikers that come strolling in from out of town. We get people from other counties and a few popular people from time to time. Families in minivans and limos alike and sometimes a few horseback riders. Never had any walk ins, too far of a trot. They all come and they are all welcome. But please wear your shoes and shirt, we ain't that kind of place. I'm not a bar and I don't sell pot. Maybe... just maybe, I hit the 'Pine every now and then, but that's it.

If you are traveling down this road, odds are you're headed to get a steak Nicole and S.O.B.S. What are S.O.B.S.? Let me tell ya. I created this fancy potato dish from left over baked potatoes, because I didn't want to waste them and throw them away. I like to make use of everything I have. I'm pretty good at being resourceful. I also take my leftover bread and make homemade croutons while cooking the potatoes. Then I get bread crumbs from that to make my crab cakes. Quite savvy I think. It just bothers me when food is wasted with so many starving children in the world. Trust me I have plenty to say about the starving and what our society could do about it, but that's a later note.

Just a note: *I hate it when someone says they are starving. Are you really?*

What do the S.O.B.S. taste like? They taste like a highly upgraded potato skin, highly I say. Some people call them sobs and other call them son-of-bitches, especially my workers who have to cook them. We sell shit loads of them and this leftover potato has become my biggest seller to date. We have to buy, scrub, wrap, cook and cut so many that I have nightmares about them. They start jumping out of the boxes, trying to escape. They grow little legs and start running across the field in their little Chuck Taylor tennis shoes. Then the cows swoop them up in their mouths and brings them to the door all covered in cud.

152

There are only a few of my nightmares that are worse. Like constantly being stalked by an alligator. Which I have had on several occasions. They say if you dream of alligators, it's a symbol of someone treacherous in your life. It says that this person has a strong hold on you despite your efforts to break free from the unhealthy relationship. There was only one person I had those dreams around, but don't worry, there gone now. Not dead, don't worry again, just gone.

I also dream all my grills disappear every time I have to cook. It's always at different locations, but always the same situation. Some of the time, I don't even have steaks to cook. The customers start to chant, "kill her" as they bang their knifes on the tables. That shit gives me panic attacks and night sweats, and when I wake up I'm exhausted.

Let's talk STEAK shall we. When walking through the parking lot you should smell the steaks on the grill. It sends a spicy aroma all across the dining room and out across the fields. I can't believe I have yet to attract every coyote in the surrounding area, but I've only seen one. I hear them at night with their barks, yips, yelps and growls, and howls while chasing their prey back behind the house. It can sound quite unnerving. I've just been waiting to walk out the door at night into a pack of them waiting to chew me to pieces.

Oh shit! I forgot to mention the steak is named after Summer. Can't believe I forgot to tell you that. It's Steak Nicole, not Steak Summer. Yes, it's my famous Missy meat, and the secret is in the marinade. It's also delicious due to the spice and some serious love and attention. Its not gourmet cooking, it's quality cooking. I've tried in the past, to teach people my methods of cooking it, but It doesn't work. Guess I'm not much of a teacher, but then again, maybe that shit just can't be taught.

They ask me. "How long do you cook it?"

"I don't know! I've never timed it."

"Do you touch it to see what temperature it is?"

"No! I never touch my meat, once it's on the grill."

"How do you know it's done?"

"I don't know! I just do."

So I guess that's why I'm still at the grill instead of doing meet and greet at the door, and talking to people. Which would be a great change of pace, instead of just being the wizard behind the curtain.

Yep! My Steak Nicole, has given Summer and I a good livin. It confuses my aunt Frankie when someone orders steak Diane. "Who's Diane?" Frankie would ask and continue to rant. "We ain't got no steak Diane here. Never have, never will, I don't think we will. Will we Missy? You planning on having another kid?"

As I laugh, "not likely Frankie."

As you know, Frankie is my dad's sister, Miss Beehive. She is only 363 days older than him, not even a year apart. She was born on January 3rd and Daddy on December 31st of the same year.

Ladies of the Luckett clan. Mom must have done been booted out. Just kidding Mom. From left to right. Nevita, Effie, Libby, Darlene, FRANKIE, Ann, Euell, and Peggy in the floor.

I use to call my Maw-maw out when she said she didn't like sex.

I was always like, "Yeah! Whatever! Two kids in the same year would prove you different."

She would reply, "Watch it kiddo! Back in those days we had to have sex when the man wanted it. It was our duty, but I never participated."

"Well! That just sucks Maw-maw. For the both of you."

Oops! Off the subject again. Back to Frankie for a moment. She came with the building. We say that, cause when I opened I hadn't a clue what I was doing. The place was so big compared to what I was use to, and I knew I couldn't do it by myself. I would stand up at the grill, and Mick would go out to a table and say. "Can you hear me now?"

She seemed so far away and all I could think is how in the hell am I gonna do this by myself. I didn't know where to look for help. Frankie was one of the first to step up and say, "I will help. I'm bored just sitting at home." She has been here helping out ever since, just helping, our little helper. She just likes getting out of the house and being around people. When we're not busy and I'm sending people home, she always begs and pleas. Please don't send me home, I just wanna stay.

She says she used to be a good woman, till she started hanging out with us whippersnappers after work. Listening to us make dirty jokes and cuss. But don't you worry, she fits right in now. She says, we broke her a long time ago. Like a wild horse tamed, she's been broken in. When she jumps in on some of our conversation, she jumps in good. Wish I could recall some of shit she comes up with. She definitely likes to joke around. She has earned the respect of the name 'Miss Frankie. Maybe, hopefully soon, I will get her on a recording.

I THINK I'LL JUST BE HAPPY TODAY

Remember folks to always joke. For if there wasn't one joke after another, what would life be? It would be mundane, so please oh Lord, don't let it stop. So around here, we laugh a lot and.... Bitch a lot. Although, 'I' of all people know that laughter is not a constant thing, it has to be maintained throughout life. Even though sometimes you don't even remember what you laughed at. Because most of the time we don't. But it's just plain healthy to keep the laughter coming. It is the best medicine ever, I mean ever. But never ever to spite another person's feelings of course, well... maybe sometimes. I've been the butt of several jokes, from being a woman, to living in Kentucky, to being a lesbian. Oh! Did I say I was a lesbian, just forget that comment. Yep, just stick it the back of your head, thanks. Let's tell a joke, just to get it off your mind.

How do you drown a blonde? Put a scratch and sniff at the bottom of the pool.

I've learned that sometimes humor can come at the most unlikely times. Like the time fireworks blew out of my house while burning down. I almost laughed then, while parachute men were flying all about the sky, but I didn't, maybe I should have. But sometimes you are just too distraught to laugh at the moment. It's hard to do while removing that wrench that got thrown into your day, it makes finding your laughter and planning your journey as hard as keeping up with twenty kids at Disney Land. It's best you get a laughter magnet, to draw in the people who bring it, in the midst of the most trying circumstances.

The people around me have brought plenty of laughter into my life. Trust me, I have the laugh lines to prove it. They have also been the reason for a few of these gray hairs, but who's counting. Point is, laugh, then laugh some more. Even when stress is trying its best to grab a hold and you feel completely spent and the curve balls just keep coming. Just take a deep breath and give it a *'barn burner'* (that would be a good country style kick in the ass.)

Joe Mack says that when he is here at the Café, it feels a lot like sex with all its frenetic activity, fast and energetic, in a rather wild and uncontrollable way. He feels like a horny Warlock amongst a coven of witches, and it's crazy as a shit house rat, and this place makes me crazy as shit house rat sometimes. It has become a monster that I have yet to tame. It can be like a zoo, without the zoo keepers.

The key, is to stay goal oriented while the bricks are piling up, because they will. Always keep a sledge hammer near, you're gonna need it, unless you want walled in and no one to laugh at. There are still times it makes me feel exhaustipated-" (too tired to give a crap anymore.)

Mom walked in the other day and handed me a packet of something. I was like, "what is this?" She said, "therapy wrist bands." I asked. "Do you have any that will fit my head." She looked at me funny and asked. "Why you need them for your head?" I rolled my eyes and said, "Really mom!" Then she giggled and said, "oh, I get it. You need some brain therapy."

But readers, when I start to feel that way, I get a card in the mail from a customer that says. *"Thanks for taking care of us at Missy's Cafe, great food!!! Great hospitality!!! Great therapy!!!"*

Or I read a blog that says.

"Don't let the name fool you!! It's a steak house not a Cafe! Let me tell you, we had a fantastic food, a fantastic server and the bartender had the best personality! The owner Missy herself is the one who cooked our steak!! Highly recommend this out of the way place! I only wish it was in Bucks County Pennsylvania.!!"

Then once again, I have to rethink my world. Yes! It's worth it. I Think I'll just be happy today. Until the next night when I hear dishes in the dish room breaking. It sounds like Zeus is throwing lighting bolts down from the heavens straight into my kitchen. It makes my ears hurt and my body cringe. I NEED THERAPY. Naw... just kidding, no wait! Maybe? Naw, I'm good, check with me next week. I think I'll just be happy today.

So yes! I'm back and fourth on my feelings almost daily. One day I may not want to give a shit, but then I do. I never try to jeopardize my place of business, no matter what distress I may be going through. The customer never knows, well, maybe the ones at the bar, only because they're right there with me, while I am completely exposed. The reason I'm exposed is the kitchen is completely open and if you sit at the bar, you're sure to be entertained.

We were moving so fast one night, that I looked up and the woman at the bar was eating just as fast and like she had just gotton out of prison. Shoveling it in like someone was gonna take it if she didn't finish quick. When I walked past her, I was laughing and she was laughing. Not sure exactly what I said to her, but I know what she said to me. "I'm eating so fast, because I feel like I need to keep up with your pace, it's just crazy back there." I asked her if she was gonna leave me a tip for the entertainment and she said. "Most definitely. It's better than dinner and a movie, so we just saved money by not going."

My point is: I hope I have some funny Cafe stories for you even though its hard to get comedy down on paper. So very, very, hard. Why? Because the joke usually lies in the delivery. It's as hard as a baby trying to crawl up a set of steps for the first time. There is so..... many had to be there moments. Wish I had a Go Pro strapped on my head, then I would just start a *You Tube* page instead. That would be way easier. The only thing I regret about any of these stories, is that someone wasn't filming it.

Maybe if I was a comedian, or maybe even a writer, this would all be easy. But who is looking for easy? ME! The rules of writing suck. But since I've been studying up on things, what I have learned about the rules of writing, is that maybe there are no rules at all. Just give you readers an enjoyable read. But what about the comedy? Damn it! Sorry! Working on it.

Life has its up and downs. No one ever masters it all, but I'm trying. Sometimes... When..... I think I am mastering things, I realize, maybe not so much. Things just start to fall apart again, but then something funny happens. Seesaw, seesaw, that shit is fun as a kid. So why not now? So once again, I think I'll just be happy today.

Real time: Dad walked in this morning and asked mom if she knew what day it was. She looked puzzled for a moment. Then she walked over to him, teased him with her smiling eyes and said. I know what day it is, it's our wedding anniversary. I loved you that day.

How do you make Lady Gaga cry? Poker face.

I'm gonna give you a booster shot so you can become immune to some of the madness here at the Cafe. I sure would have appreciated one fifteen years ago. Let's turn some nonsense into entertainment. Just some stuff that has happened this past week. You can believe me or not, no one has your hands tied behind your back. Just know that you could talk to anyone around here and they could tell you, I honestly could never get that many people to lie.

Just the other day Mom was cleaning out the fridge, while still in her pajamas of course. She loves to come over and clean in those things. Then the phone rang. I went to answer it and when I looked at the caller ID, it said that the Cafe was calling. Keep in mind, I'm in the Cafe. While the phone is still ringing, I'm trying to hand it to

Mom, as I'm trying to get to my cell phone to take a picture. Mom kinda didn't know what was going on, neither did I for that matter, but for two different reasons.

About that time my order guy came in the door. He always walks in nice and smooth all dressed up with a smile on his face and a computer in his hand. My mom thinks he has the sexiest butt ever. But anyway, I say to him. "OMG Jason, you're not gonna' believe this."

"What?"

"Look at the phone, this is the Cafe number! How does the Cafe number, call the Cafe number? My phone called my phone. Just doesn't make any sense."

"Was it Walter?" As he starts to laugh.

"Ha-ha, I hope not, but I'm thinking maybe. It's just so weird. I never know if it's him, power surges or just freaking life."

"Do you have a phone at your house?" As he sits down at the bar.

"No! I mean I have phone lines, but no phones hooked up. There are two things since the house burnt down I decided on. Not to hook the phone back up over there and I've chosen not to purchase underwear.

He leans back and continues to laugh "You mean to tell me you've been going commando for over five years now?"

"Yep! And a little longer, my house burnt in 08. Just sit there and chill for a second and quit picturing me with no panties on. Let me tell you everything that has happened just this week."

"Luckily I have the time and the interest." he said.

Then mom walks past with the mop. Jason takes a look and asked, "does she always wear those?"

"Most of the time, I do to when I can, just never in public. I don't do the Walmart thing."

"I'm sure you don't." as he winked. "What was you gonna tell me?"

"Well, first of all, last Friday after work my feet were hurting so bad, I could hardly walk. Then when I got home and took my socks off, my two big toes were fucking black."

Mom looks up like I dropped a bombshell. "Watch your mouth!"

"Oh! Get over it Mom."

"I'm serious Missy, that's not lady like in front of Jason here."

"I'm use to it, no harm no foul. You should have heard my wife the other day. I sent her into one of your guys nasty liquor stores, I got it on message and I didn't erase it, here listen."

Mom puts the mop down and walks over and starts to listen. "OMG! Does your wife really cuss like that?"

"Oh Mom! You cuss too."

"You're damn right I do." As we all started to laugh, then mom went back to mopping. She seemed to be doing a little dance with it, maybe to get Jason's attention.

Jason reaches over and grabs my arm. "Missy, back to your toes. You may wanna wash them."

"Whatever Jason, they have been washed. Somebody was trying to tell me I've probably got diabetes or something."

"Well, let's hope not."

"I'm headed to the toe doctor next week. Let me finish my story. It has been a cluster fuck around here. My deep fryer went out and the pool people came and said I had six holes in my pool.

"Six?"

"Yep, six. Then on Wednesday when I came into work, UPS delivered a big ass package and I knew it wasn't mine. I thought maybe Summer ordered something, so I told him to just leave the damn thing. So when Sara, one of my workers came in, we just stood there and stared at it like, should we open it. So we did, It was a sound bar."

"What the hell is a sound bar?"

"We were wondering the same thing. So I decide to call my credit card company and they said it was from Groupon. So then I called Groupon, blah blah blah and they said I had another one on the way. I was like, do what? They said, yes, you ordered them from your iphone. I asked her, how is that possible? I didn't order them. Then she said, well ma'am, you could have thrown your phone in your purse and it may have ordered it. I told her I get that, but for starters I don't carry a purse and for second it ordered twice on two different days. So how is that possible?"

"Well, Missy, either somebody is messing with you or your ghost are. Do they need a sound bar, to communicate."

"They might, they've been trying to communicate in other ways. But anyway Jason, you get my point. You wanna' hear more?" as I laughed.

"I would love to, even though it's a complaint; I'm finding it strangely funny."

Mom throws the mop down again and comes walking toward us. "Jason, my husband is in the hospital, what about that? I've been up there all week, running back and fourth, then stopping down my mom's and helping her, in her ninety year old stage."

"I know Mom, that's terrible and I hate it for Jo Eddie. He feels awful I know, I'm gonna have to take him a pie."

"Really sorry to hear that Marceline." Jason replies.

"I know it's happening to Jo Eddie, but for some reason, everything that happens effects this place and Missy somehow."

"How is that?" Jason asks.

"Cause, I can't be here to help my little poky bear."

I looked at Mom and said, "you make sure you take care of what you need to. I'm good."

"I need to take care of you. I hate it when this effects you and you have to take care of everything."

"Jason, she only says that because I have to depend on workers to be here. Cause when something happens in their lives, it affects this place and really puts me in a bind."

Mom raises her voice and says, "they're always putting you in a bind Missy."

Jason replies, "That's what you get for being an entrepreneur Missy."

I look at him. "Yeah, yeah, Jason. Sometimes their excuses are so lame it's ridiculous. Like the excuse, my dad let the dog out and I got to go get it. I use to get so mad that I could have bit a nail in half. Now I say whatever and walk away, but not reacting is as hard as getting into a Slim Jim."

"That's pretty freakin' hard."

"Jason, I've been open almost fifteen years and I've only missed one night of work and that's the day my house burnt down."

"Really!" he said.

"Yep! Really! And I'm gonna finish my venting. You still got time to hear the rest? I know your giving me free rein, so just tell me when you need me to stop."

"Please proceed."

"So Thursday night, I'm over here working and Summers friend calls me from Summers phone. They think the house in Louisville is

165

on fire. I start to panic, thinking what am I gonna do? While I'm running around in a panic trying to finish cooking the food, she sends me a video of the fire department arriving. Three big fire trucks sitting in front of the house. I'm running around like a chicken with its head off in a panic and not able to leave work or do a damn thing about it."

"I bet you were a nervous wreck."

"I was. My dad was sitting here, right where you're sitting and I was telling him about the fire and he said all calm and shit, just tell them to call the fire department. I said they already did. Then my Dad says, don't burn my fish. It took a minute for that to sink in. Then he went and sat at a table with some people he knew. Oh! It made me so mad. I was ready to blow a fuse and I was gonna tell him about it. But I got so busy and he left before I got to let him have it for being so nonchalant. I know he couldn't have done anything either, but damn! Seem a little concerned, when you think your daughters house is burning down, especially while your granddaughter is in it."

Jason starts to laugh again.

"Hold on, that's not all. You know that I'm trying to write this series of books, right. So I'm trying to figure out how to publish. So I've been studying up on every thing and I find out that Amazon is having a huge dispute with authors and book companies. I'm telling ya, it's wearing me out."

"That's all too crazy Missy."

"Hold... on! Jason, that's not all"

"Holy shit! There is more? Are you lying to me right now?"

"No! I'm not. Last Saturday I finally sold my Katie Perry ticket to Logan's friend and I promised him they were good, because I bought them on Stub Hub. He was worried and I assured him they

166

were perfectly fine. Mom, Summer, Logan and I, were gonna go, but I have to work, because you know of course my cook fell through. Mom can't go because Jo Eddie has been in the hospital. So anyway, about six thirty I get a text. "Hey this is Logan. Tickets are a scam! We can't get in. Summer is on the phone with Stub Hub" Jason....13.... hundred... dollars worth of tickets! I couldn't believe it. But right before that happened, I was trying to download the tickets from my Yahoo account. This thing came up saying Yahoo mail was down. How often does that fucking happen? I mean really. I took a picture of it, look!"

"Damn Missy."

"No Jason, Hold on little doggy. I have more and I really don't know what's going on right now. I was sitting upstairs writing the other night and the radio in the bathroom came on. It was about one in the morning. I just calmly reached for my phone, nice... and easy.... and text Summer. *'the radio in your bathroom just came on."* Then she text me back, *'Mom get out of the house NOW! It's possessed.'*

"I take it, she has had run ins with Walter."

"Of course. I will have to tell you about all that later, but I was quite bothered. I texted back *'I think they're just having a dance'* and she text back *'oh,,, OK LOL.'*

"What do you think made your radio come on?" He asked.

"Hell, I don't know. Shit like that happens all the time."

"You might need to get out."

"Naw, I'm good, I think. It's just disturbing sometimes. Don't think their evil or anything."

"Anything else?"

"Well, beings you asked. After work the other night, Sara, Mandy and me were sitting here at the bar. Sara kinda took a deep breath. We asked, what's wrong Sara? She said, I've just had a rough day. Then Mandy in her little pouty voice asked. Why? What happened? Sara was bleating like a lost kitten. Well... I was at Walmart..... and I got in line, the lady was taking so long. She was couponing and my ice cream was gonna melt. I started to laugh, is that it, Sara? She was like No! On the way home I got behind this little old lady and had to pass her. I looked at Mandy and said. I have to pass someone every day and started to laugh. Mandy said, that's it? Then Sara is like, no you guys! Then I dropped the milk when I got home and I had to lay a towel down."

Jason said, "She really thought she had a rough day, didn't she?"

"She did. Look Jason, then Mandy starts to mix a drink and asked. You need a drink Sara? That sounds pretty rough. Then we busted out laughing again. Then Sara said why you guys laughing? I looked at Mandy and said. Damn! I wish my ice cream would melt. Then Sara looked at me and asked, Why Miss? As I giggled and said, you really want me to start? As they both shook their heads yes. Then I told them everything I'm telling you, excluding the sound bar. Sara was here for that. Then Sara goes, I feel bad for complaining now."

Jason wiped his forehead and shook out his shirt. "That is funny, bet she did feel like shit."

"Yep, last couple days when we walk past her we say is your ice cream melting. Oh... and I had told them about the Pepsi Machine, ice machine and fridge over there. They have all messed up in the past three weeks. Is it my luck, or the damn ghost? I just wanna know."

Wiping his brow with his thumb. "I don't know Missy, but I really hate to laugh at your misfortune. Is it hot in here or is it just me? Is your air out?"

"I hope the hell not and go ahead and laugh, that's all I can do these days. This shit happens all the time. It's gonna be the straw one of these days, just the straw, then your gonna be taking my order from nut house." as I walked over to check the air.

Then at that very moment I got a text. It was from a friend and it said, 'Missy I just pissed Pam off. Don't think we will be out tonight.' My face just went blank, I thought it was gonna be the straw.

"What?" Jason asked.

"Do you really want me to tell ya?"

"Yep! sure do."

"Well, this girl was suppose to edit my book, and my friend just pissed her off. Holy shit! Just go ahead and take my order. Damn!"

"Are you sure?"

"Yep! We better before something happens." Then I scream, "the fucking air is not working."

"Yes, you're right, I might wanna get on out of here. This is getting ugly."

"Oh yeah, you wanna know what else before I call my air man. My new knives were falling apart Saturday. I just bought them and people were getting them little screws in their plates. Thought before the night was over I might get sued, I'm so over this bullshit. Am I being sabotaged by something? I just need to know."

"Obviously something Missy." Then he took my order, folded up his laptop, and said "good luck with the air" and left.

Sshhhhhheeeeewwwwwllllllllllllll Yep! This place will drive you berserk. That's why I sometimes lose motivation and my priorities change. Then shortly after that, Sara walks in with a really long face and tells me her boyfriend just got hit by a train, but that he was gonna okay. Then she said, I sure wish my ice cream was melting at this point. All I could reply was, well you upped me this week and we both started to laugh.

FYI: *If you can't find the humor in it, you haven't dealt with it yet.*

Just a note: *"They say that other people can't control your emotions, I call bullshit."*

I'm wondering if this next quote fits, not sure. Maybe.

Quote: *"Life is a series of natural and spontaneous changes. Don't resist them; that only creates sorrow. Let reality be reality. Let things flow naturally forward in whatever way they like. --Lao Tzu.--*

Is this real life right now? Is this the natural order they are talking about? I don't think so, this is something out of the realm of just normal and natural. Stuff like this can't just continue to happen all the time.

Sometimes all I wanna do is escape to a peaceful world, the one that hides inside my head. Why can't life be like the *Calgon* commercials. "The heat! The cat! The dog! The workers! The baby! The ghost! That does it! *Calgon* take me away" and poof there you is. Even if you escape and loose your cares to your tub full of bubbles, it can never last any longer than 30 minutes, or you turn to a prune. So, I just create a place in my head, until I find such a lasting place, cause nobody wants to be a prune.

When I told Summer I wanted a cabin in the woods, it upset her for some reason. Now I really don't get why. Why would she have a problem with me wanting to become stress free and get away from

170

all the exchaustipating things? Does she really think I'm trying to get away from her? Maybe! Of course I'm not, but I feel, she thinks that. Maybe she's young and doesn't understand. My mom said, of course she doesn't understand, this is her home and she wants to come home to it. Then I turned to Mom and asked, where is my home? She pondered for a moment, then said, that's not nice. Then we both laughed.

But when I think about it, the woods that is. Where would the laughter come from? It takes people to make that happen. I mean maybe I could laugh at the squirrels or the raccoons, but not likely. Maybe, just maybe, I have to deal with all things around me, to stand by and hold on just for the funny shit. So as good as the cabin sounds, I need people, people need people.

I remember when I used to look at my pictures or videos, I would laugh so hard. So many fun things we did. But sometimes it's really hard to pull all those memories to the surface without them. I could have made an awesome picture book, which would have been much easier than this. PICTURES!!! I need my pictures please.

Quote: "When I thought I couldn't go on, I forced myself to keep going. My success is based on persistence, not luck." - Estee Lauder

Quote: One day she finally grasped that unexpected things were always going to happen in life. And with that she realized the only control she had was how she chose to handle them. So she made the decision to survive using courage, humor and grace. She was the Queen of her own life and the choice was hers. - Lupytha Hermin

HAPPY AS A LARK

Things I sometimes feel, think or do:

Sometimes; I get totally excited when I find the right change to fit the moment.

Sometimes; When you're in your forties, it's okay to have random sixteen year old moments.

Sometimes; I forget to eat. Don't worry, Dr. said it's okay and that the Cavemen did it for years.

Sometimes; I get ecstatic just because my can of mountain dew was ice cold and I look up and thank the stars above.

Sometimes; I wish living didn't feel like it was gonna kill me.

Sometimes; I know it's just life.

Sometimes; I like being the container, because the container can't be contained.

Sometimes; I flick my boogers out the window. Better than eating them, like the girl in grade school. So you can get disgusted if you want, but only if you have never picked a booger while driving. Now come on, I know you have. Where did you put it? Sara says she rolls them into little balls like me, which I feel most people do, seems normal enough. So to be sure, we asked Mandy. What do you do with your boogers when you're in the car? Put them in a napkin she said. But what if you don't have a napkin we asked. I shake it out the window. But what if it sticks? I roll it in a little ball, till it flies off. Exactly! I said. Case proven.

Sometimes; I get really aggravated when a fly gets in the Cafe. I just say, "fly! I don't feel like fucking with you today." And yes sometimes; I talk to flies.

172

Sometimes; When that brave little fly lands on my arm. I break out the fly swatter and smash it on its little head and say, NOW! Be brave little f**ker. Sometimes; That's what crazy looks like. Luckily I know when I'm being crazy and yes that is crazy. Talking to flies is crazy.

Sometimes: Things just loop in my head all day long, same thought over and over again. Neurological loop. Drives me freakin' nuts. It's like trying to get away from a fly trapped in your car. Why do I keep talking about flies? Because I live in the damn country, and they're everywhere.

Sometimes; I'm smarter than the average bear and sometimes I want to be eaten by a bear, but we will discuss that theory later. Hold up! Breaking news! Be careful what you wish for. There was a bear just spotted in Raywick. Hopefully it's not on its way to get me. If these stories end, you will know why.

And....Sometimes...... I wish I was just a dumb blonde.

Sometimes; I feel like I have the memory of a goldfish, oh poor little goldfish, that was so bad of me.

Sometimes; I appreciate ignorance, because ignorance is bliss for a reason.

Sometimes; I wanna know what it's like, not to know. Know what you ask? Well lots of things. You know, stuff like world hunger, betrayal, lies, murder, stress, cheatin' hearts and so on.

Sometimes; I walk over to the Cafe and walk into unexpected conversations. Like this one between my Mom and Beverly.

Now readers, I want you to picture Karen from *Will and Grace* while reading this conversation and mom is Karen. If you don't know who Karen is, I recommend you set the book down and google a skit of her from the show. Highly recommend. The rest of this chapter is also intended for adult audiences only.

I hear Mom in her high pitched voice. "There she goes ejaculating! They said she was just... in heaven..... Artificial insemination with the kangaroos were just plum... ridiculous........I thought I was gonna! Well, I was just sitting there, and the Koala bears. Oh my God! I can't wait to tell Joe Eddie."

I was squinting trying to see who she was talking to, because my eyes were still trying to adjust from the sunlight. I was also trying to grasp what kind of conversation I was walking into. "Tell Joe Eddie what?" I said.

Mom is really trying to get my attention, flapping her arms all around, ignoring my question. "Look; they were showing it up real close. Trying to open up her little vagina... her thing was about like this." As mom pinched her fingers together. "And they showed a kangaroo dick, it was about this long. Never seen so much stuff going on in all my life."

I'm just standing there thinking. What in the hell kinda of conversation did I walk in on? Then I hear Beverly say, "The one where they open the vagina reminds me of Logan's story yesterday."

Who is Logan you ask? Well let's introduce him! Just a small preview. Don't want to bombard you with adjectives, only because if someone starts to bombard me with adjectives, I end up not being interested in what they have to say at all.

Yes, Logan! He is Summers friend. They went to school together and eventually he became my friend. Then became Moms friend after he worked at the Cafe. He was attending nursing school at the time. He is now a nurse. He is eccentric, full of bubbles and somewhat of a country version of Liberace. He and my mom have the dynamic of Jack and Karen from *Will and Grace*. I would give anything to have had a video camera on them over the years, while having their morning coffee. I would be rich and retired. They are a mess, and put stitches in my side at times. They are purty funny.

Summer and Logan

But anyway, I will let Beverly continue her story. She goes on to say. "He had a woman that weighed about 400 pounds trying to put a thing up her, whatever you call it. And he kept telling her to spread them. I said Logan what do you think when your doing that?"

Beverly starts laughing and I'm still trying to figure out the conversation.

Mom smacks the bar top. "Go on Beverly, what was you gonna say?"

"Then he said, well I'm real nice while I'm doing it. But I would rather them to be in ICU, I don't like being talked to. I want my patients to be on ventilators and sedated. Is he crazy or what?"

I giggled. "Logan, he is something else. I gave him a cupcake the other night when he was over the house. You know, those hostess things down Blandford's store. When he put it in his mouth, he was like OMG! What kind is this? It is so moist, I swear if a woman's vagina tasted like this, I might lick it."

Beverly starts to laugh "I can't wait to tell him about the bear and the Kangaroos. He is so funny."

Mom jumps right back in, totally ignoring our story. She was so excited. "That show last night, I was so shocked. They would get that Koala Bear, I mean they would get up this close. That little ole koala bear a grinnin, just happy as a lark. And then they stick a tube up in there, and there she goes..."

I decide to ram-sack the conversation. Just to get mom off this subject. "Hey listen! Two girls were heading to Disney Land, the sign read. Disney Land Left. Then they both cried and turned around and drove home."

Then there was silence. You could have heard a pen drop in cotton. Then Beverly finally started to laugh.

Mom still looked dumbfounded. "I don't get it." Then we all started to laugh.

Beverly looks at Mom. "Disney land left. They are no longer in the vicinity. They thought it left Marceline."

"Okay! Okay! I get it." Mom said.

176

Beverly stared at me and said, "Poor blondes get it all the time don't they Missy?"

"Don't be looking at me. It's not the true blonds that are dingy, it's the ones that have colored it that way. They dingy from all the chemicals."

Back at it again with her voice pitchy and high, mom blurts out. "This kangaroo, I'm telling ya. Female kangaroo! They got up close on camera. I don't know even how they did it. They said they was having a hard time. But that dick is trying to find it, well... they said penis. The PENIS is trying to find it. When he finally gets it in, here comes another male kangaroo knocking him off. He had her pulled to him so tight. The other kangaroo is hitting him with his head." as mom was gritting her teeth and acting it out.

I finally asked "What the hell was you watching?"

As mom ignored me. "Listen! I didn't miss a second of it. Listen Missy, then I told Beverly, a minute ago, before you walked in. I got finished watching it and I went and got my vibrator."

As Beverly and I busted out laughing. "Do What?"

Mom was getting excited while saying this. "And you know what? You know how long it took me."

As Beverly cuts in and shuts Mom down for a millisecond. "Missy if she brings any strange animals over, I'm gonna be worried."

Moms voice was getting louder and louder, "I swear Missy! I touched myself with it, and there... I went. They ain't got nothing over on me."

Beverly laughs. "If we see a Great Dane or any kind of odd animals, we will know. We will know, won't we Missy."

"We sure will."

Mom slung her arms up in the air. "Can you imagine that man trying to push that little thing in there, and there she went. It was hilarious..."

Beverly moves the conversation to her little beagle hound who has one leg missing. She said, "Let me change the subject and tell ya'll about my little dog. We called it Nubit and somebody wanted to breed it to its female. So Ricky and them built a little stool so it could lean on it, you know, with what little bit of leg it had. Well it still couldn't get it going. So they had to get its little penis.....and put it up in the female dog. I walked out, I said this is too embarrassing."

Mom jumped right back in, "oh I couldn't take my eyes off the TV for a second."

"They do horses like that sometimes." Beverly said.

"I know" Mom replies. "But to watch their hands and making them do it. This one man said, oh, it didn't hit the tube. It's all over my hands. Imagine getting that stuff on your hands."

Beverly once again changes the subject as Mom gets up to use the bathroom. "Let me tell you about my pig real quick. He was the best, but he like to make love to the water trough. I got a picture of it."

You could hear Mom in the background yelling, "that pig was this big and he was black and white, wasn't he Beverly?"

"But anyway Missy, he kept turning the water trough over. So, we had to get him a new one and I come out one day and yelled, Porky! He is just laying on top of it and I thought he was dead! He is not moving, I was getting really upset and I yelled Porky! Porky! Finally, he jumps up, I didn't think any thing about it. Well... I come out a few days later and he is just going to town on it, I mean going to town. I couldn't catch him that day. He got done before I could grab my camera, but I watched him. Then he laid on top of it, you know, just flopped on it. So the next few times I took a camera and caught him in action. I sent a picture to Joe Keith and Jimmy with a note that said, here's my Porkis with his Steel Magnolia. Jimmy Bickett didn't get it, that silly fool. But, Joe Keith did."

Get the picture

I pointed at mom. "Just like the joke a minute ago, one of you got it and the other didn't."

Mom standing there with her chicken legs, puts her hand on her slender hips. "Well let me tell you this real fast. I mean this woman was excited about this story. That kangaroo was by this big tree."

I looked at Beverly. "OMG! She is back on the kangaroo shit again."

179

Beverly stood up. "No wonder your Mom was beating those pigs with a broom, she was jealous and horny."

Mom was too excited to even hear what Beverly just said and continues on with her rant. "And it would come around the tree playing with the other one, and the lady on the show would say look how they are playing around. Went on for 45 minutes. He would come around this way, then she would go around that way, they were acting just like people. The female was obviously playing hard to get, but then she finally gave up. Ya'll have got to watch this *Sex in the Wild*, I never seen anything like that on TV. Oh well, I guess I better head home and change my cloths. I will come back over and do the onions in the morning, unless! Beverly, you wanna cut them?"

Beverly replied, "I'm not cutting any, I'm not cutting my hand off." Then they both walked out the door. Conversation over.

"Sometimes I lie awake at night, and I ask, 'Where did I go wrong'. Then a voice says to me, "This is going to take more than one night." --Charles M. Schulz--

GET USE TO IT

Let's talk about Jimmy, you know, Mr. Heart Attack. He was telling me about his experience when he first started working over here.

This is Jimmy speaking and explaining it to me.

"When I first started workin' with ya, I was workin' the grill there, and I was scraping it. Something flew up and hit me in the eye and I said, "God dang it!" Then Liz looked over at me and said.

180

"What is it Jimmy? I said, "I got something in my darn eye over here." Liz replied. "well, Jimmy, you better get use to it, boss here, makes you work no matter what's wrong with ya" So, later on that night she burnt herself and started bitching, she was yelping like a dog. I looked over at her and started to laugh and said, "Get use to it, Liz." Then, I thought to myself, "That shit is funny."

Keep in mind, Jimmy probably finds a lot of things funny after getting out of prison, he is pretty simple and a free spirit. But he tells some pretty elaborate tales, even on himself. I guess that's what he did for entertainment while stuck in there all those years. We'll catch back up on him later.

So Yes! I agree...I can be a little bit like *Gordon Ramsay* at times. A little tough and louder than I should be. Only because, I'm trying to get it right for my customer. I am tough (not mean) and think other people should be too. Mom isn't the only tator' hard to peel. I get burns, cuts and hot particles off the grill in my eyes all the time. I have even sliced the end of my finger nearly off with a meat slicer. It was right before opening hours, when I ran my finger through that damn thing, I instantly grab my finger tight and took off running in circles around the bar, as Mom and one of my workers gave chase trying to stop me. I was leaving a blood trail everywhere. I guess I thought by running I would escape my injury. I swear they said I ran around the counter at least five times before I stopped and finally headed to the sink. That's when I noticed a large portion of my finger was barely hanging on. I jumped in my car, drove to town to get it stitched back on and came right back to work. So call me what you will, I call it tough.

So anyway, in August it gets hotter than a Witch's cunt in here, especially back here with the grills. Yes, I know, cunt is a very vulgar word, just expressing how hot it gets. I would like to say it's a Freudian slip, but it wasn't. When my workers start to complain about the heat, I grab them, put their hand over my grill for just a second. "Say something now, leave or get use to it."

Quick story about a for real Freudian slip: *I was sitting at a bar with a mutual friend. She was three sheets in the wind. When she looked up at the bartender and ordered a hairy pussy. The bartender looked at me with confusion. Then I said, I think maybe she wants a fuzzy navel. I thought to myself, or maybe, she wants what she ordered.*

So a few years back I had a four wheeler wreck. I usually get straight up from my spills and falls. Not so much this day. I was down for the count and that my friend, just usually don't happen. I'm usually up as quick as I hit the ground, except for the splitting the head incident.

We were once again headed out on Kathleen and Danny's annual horse ride over in Shit Creek. Yep! It's a place around here. I'm sure to tell ya about some ventures on that old dirt road.

It was very cold that day. We all had on winter jackets and gloves. Before we left, Karrie handed me a drinking pack. "Here, you might need this since you will be driving. I think its pretty cool. See, you just fill it here with your liquor, put it on your back and sip through this tube." as she held it up to her mouth.

"Thanks, Karrie. That's pretty cool, hands free drinking. I like that. I will put some whiskey in it to keep me warm."

We were on four wheelers instead of horses. A little over halfway though the day we stopped up on top of Scotts Ridge, by the big WB tower, to listen to Danny and them play music. My cousin Karrie, came rolling up with mud on her from head to toe. All you could see were her pearly whites. It was like another Orbits commercial, dirty mouth? Clean it up. Ding.

"Where the hell did you get into all that mud?" I asked with excitement.

"Over there in the woods, there is a path. It's pretty sweet."

It was a Spur-of-the-moment adventure. "Oh shit! I got to do this. Let's go muddin' people."

"Missy be careful. You don't wanna be hurting anyone this year." Someone said.

"Yeah, who is it gonna be this year?" Karrie said, as she laughed.

"Whatever!" as I rolled my eyes. "It was years ago when I got hurt and you guys act like it happens every year."

"You broke Jimmy's foot last year."

"That wasn't my fault, he pulled right out in front of me."

"Well, just be careful, your pretty accident prone. Here I will lead the way."

"Ten four." I said.

So I hopped on my four wheeler and a friend got on the back and we took off wide open. I was following Karrie as I watched her fly through the terrain. I was right on her heels and the rest of the clan behind me. I sped up to make a splash. Instead of making the water splash, I made a splash of myself when I hit the puddle. Mary, who was behind us, said we looked like two toothpicks flying across the handle bars. I felt the impact when I hit the ground face first. My arms were sprawled out, face in the mud. Then, I felt a second vibration, instantly. It was my friend, she had landed on top of me. I

183

laid there in the puddle unable to move. My friend rolled off of me. She was okay, because obviously I broke her fall. Everyone came running over to me. Mary, rolled me over onto my back, my mouth was full of muddy water.

"Can you move? Can you move?" she asked.

I tried to talk but the mud was too thick, "gi me wat," I mumbled. To my surprise she understood what I said and immediately started pouring water in my mouth. She was sticking her fingers in there trying to get out the mud. The water was over flowing all over my face and I was gagging. "This is hor-gig-ri-ble" I began to choke. "Where is my to-bog-gan? My hair feels like it's all over the place."

Mary looks at me with a strange look. "Why you worried about your toboggan?"

I was still gargling muddy water. "I just want it! Put it on my head!"

She was trying to hold me up out of the puddle. "Well, alrighty then, will do. Can you move? You wanna roll over and try to spit it out."

I struggled to answer, "I don't think so." I laid there on display for quite awhile as people begun gathering around.

I asked Mary as I laid there trembling and in some serious pain. "Can you please, ask these people to leave?"

She turned toward the crowd and yelled. "Hey! Can all of you that's not involved with this party or this situation, just get the hell out of here."

I finally slowly got up. My drinking back pack all in tact, but I was covered in mud from head to toe. I didn't even have my pearly whites. It had to look like I ate mud pie for lunch. The grit in my

184

mouth was disgusting. "I need to spit." As I was grunting and groaning in pain.

"Spit then." Karrie said.

"It hurts to much to move."

"Somebody put her on the four-wheeler." Karrie said.

Lucky for me I had filled my backpack with Crown before the ride. I hadn't drank much of it yet, but now, it sure was going to be handy for the pain. Just like back in the cowboy days. We were about six or seven miles away from my place. No ambulance was gonna be called today, I wasn't going to allow it. One of Mary's friends drove me down on the four-wheeler. It was a very cold and painful ride. I sucked on that back pack line like it was an I.V. connection.

When they got me home, I was already a little tipsy. They kept asking me if I was okay. I told them I would be fine as I continued to groan. They really wanted to take me to the hospital, but I refused.

"Miss, you really look like you are in pain." Mary said.

"Um, I'm okay. I will go to the doctor tomorrow." even though I was feeling extreme apprehension. "You gals go ahead and head back to Louisville, it's getting late. Can you please, get me those pain pills out of the drawer before you leave. It will at least dull the throbbing."

It takes a lot for me to take a pain pill, but they were left over from when I had a tooth implant. That's a whole nother' story, on why I had no front.... tooth. If you wanna know, I will tell ya. No! Let's wait. Enough A.D.D. For now.

Before they left, they helped me change my clothes, gave me the pills and situated me on the couch. Soon I was out like a light. The next morning when I awoke in the same spot, I swear, I couldn't move. It was awful. I found myself just staring at the ceiling. I rolled around back and fourth, moaning and groaning till I finally rolled myself to the edge of the couch. Then I rolled off, peaking between the couch and ottoman. How the hell Was I gonna get up from here? I finally pulled myself up and headed to the Cafe. If anyone would have been watching, they would have sworn I was a zombie. I still had mud smeared all over my face, my shoulder was slumped and my arms were hanging straight down. I was dragging my leg and moving at turtle pace as a walked across the yard. I probably resembled something from the 'Night of the Living Dead' and looking for some brains to eat. I barely got in the door, when Mom looked up with alarm. "What the hell happened to you?"

"Mom, I desperately need you to take me to the doctor."

She turned me right back around and out the door, "get in the car, get in the car" opened the door and plopped me in the seat and off we went. I had X- rays taken and they told me nothing was broken. So I thought, cool, great, awesome. I accepted the information and grunted my way back to the car. I worked at the Cafe that weekend, suffering through the pain. I thought my shoulder was just bruised and I had to deal with it. Yep, that's what I said. Deal with it, get use to it, whatever.

When the second Saturday rolled around, it was quite a different story. I never leave my post at the grill, unless something is really up. The pain was becoming unbearable. I was wearing a ball cap and as I walked away from the grill, I pulled my cap down, so no one could see the tears. WTF.. why isn't this getting better as I started to cry. I ran and hid in the storage room, but obviously not a good hiding place, because Steph soon found me. "Miss, what's up? Are you OK?"

"I just can't take it! I can't!" But in that very instant, I sniffled up. Wiped my arm across my nose and headed back to the grill and finished up the night. Yes! I made a stop at the sink first. I washed my hands, I always do. Just got a little ahead of myself.

-Crying can be a good thing. It's a physical way to say you have had enough- HpLyrikz/Tumblr

Next day! Doctor said, a bone was broken for sure! I had never had a broken bone before. It was a broken shoulder, right in the ball of it. They had missed it at the other doctor's office. So yes, I had been working with a broken bone. The doctor told me to take eight weeks off. Now we know that's not gonna happen. So I continued to work, but with a little more care to my shoulder. Now, you know my job requirement is to flip steaks all night long. So this wasn't an easy task for me, but I did it anyway. So yes, GET USE TO IT. So ladies and gents, that's my shoulder story. That's what my ex aunt Kathy has been trying to fix with her massages. Oh, and one other thing, but haha, you know I can't tell you at the moment.

Anybody ready for a blonde joke, that was all just a little too much pain in that story.

"Three blondes walk into a building. You'd think one would've seen it."

WORKING WITH IDIOTS

Well, let me start with this. I just read an article that said working with idiots can kill you. Yes! Kill you! I have had my share to walk through the door wanting a job. As you may know I am an Aquarius.

I am creative and I love what I do. What I don't love doing, is telling people what to do. It's just part of my damn job, and I hate it. Especially when idiots come through the door wanting me to hire them. Some of them get weeded out, but some have slid on through the crack.

Trying to get workers to do what you want is painful. They say trying to control the behaviors of others is as fatal as teaching a snake to walk. *sssssssss*.

I need my Cafe to run a certain way and I want to give people a chance and a job, when needed. But, good...God, please! Why the idiots? Who dropped you off and didn't pick you back up.

In fact, according to researchers at Sweden's Lindbergh University Medical Centre, reveals that those dopes can kill you. They are as hazardous to your health as cigarettes, caffeine or greasy food. Holy shit! Who knew? So working with them on a daily basis could send you six feet under. Stress is one of the top causes of heart attacks. Maybe that's why Jimmy had one, working over here with all of us, because he was one healthy looking motherfucker.

I don't know if this next story is stressful or just plain out ridiculous. But you better believe it was an idiot move. So I'm at work and I hand a young gentleman an oven mitt and ask him to scrape my grill. The grill brush is sitting right beside him. Then I looked away for one moment to do something else. Then I hear someone yelling "FIRE!" I turn back around and the mitt is on fire and still on his hand. "Pull the mitt off you fool." I screamed. "Are you several sticks short of a bundle?" Someone else screamed.

Why on earth would he choose to scrape it with the mitt on his hand instead of with the grill brush. I will never know the answer to that question. Puts a new name to the word idiot. But it was so... stupid, that none of us could do anything but laugh. You know those

188

moments where you almost have to say bravo for being so stupid. He must have heard what the workers were saying. Readers, I'm sure you can imagine what it was with out me telling you. Let's just say he never returned to work.

Haley

Now don't get me wrong, because I love this little young one here. She is our own little homegrown Haley. I've practically helped raise her because she has always hung out with Summer. When she got old enough, she started working for me. She has eyes that look like that of a deer, human version of Bambi, precious, innocent and pure. But sometimes we truly wonder what's going on behind them. You can't help but to love her. She is not an idiot per-say, but just has idiot moments like the rest of us. She just has a few more than her share and gets away with it. Sometimes the hamster isn't in the wheel.

Example anyone? How about her trying to open a huge can of cheese, that's in an aluminum can. It requires a can opener of course. But on the top of it, it has a tab, that says (pull here) Obviously it's for easy removal after you have opened the can. When she sees the pull tap, in her mind, she absolutely thought that is how you open it. Then she said, "Oh my God! Why didn't this top pull off? I pulled the sticker off and it's not budging. How are we gonna have cheese? I don't understand Missy."

Now I don't know if a regular person would think that a piece of paper that says pull, would open a gallon tin can of cheese. But this youngster did. It was another laugh out loud moment.

"Really! Is that how you thought you opened that?" One waitress said.

Haley starts to huff as she walks off. "I was just having a blonde moment you guys."

A waitress starts to laugh. "Looks like you're missing a couple grapes from your vine."

You could see the embarrassment on Haley's face as her cheeks turned red. "Whatever! It's not like you haven't ever been a couple steps short of a staircase yourself bitches."

We all started *snaughling*. You know, that moment where you're laughing so hard you snort, then laugh because you snorted, then snort because you laughed. Yep, that's what we did.

I could go on and on at this moment, but I won't. Even though I'm dying to tell you about the time she knitted a sweater for her chicken. Yes, she has chicken pets.

I mean most of this idiotic stuff keeps us cracking up. Till it comes down to crunch time in the Cafe, then things get a little more serious. Because they do around six o'clock every Saturday night. The place gets packed as a can of sardines. Everyone has their own task, but team work always works the best. It's a hard load to pull sometimes, especially when there are ones who are doing really stupid things. It starts to back up service, then the laughter stops temporarily. I, myself, can't do a lot about it. I am stuck on the grill cooking steaks, hundreds of them most of the time. I'm stuck like peanut butter to the side of a jar. Even though I'm moving so fast you can't see my limbs, maybe like a human hummingbird. Boy what I wouldn't give to be an octopus. No, a hummingpus. I could really get some shit done then. You might wonder, could my brain keep up with that? Of course it could, for now anyway.

I own the place and I don't even have the luxury to walk around and check on everything like I would like to. It's either cook the steaks or walk around apologizing to the customers the whole night. So I just choose to stay at the grill and cook the steaks like my customers want me to. I'm sorry.....I'm not the best at running a Cafe... but I care, and that means a lot in the food business. Success depends on how your food goes out and why people come back and wait two hours for a steak.

I have a tendency to tell my workers, that I am only responsible for what I say. I'm not responsible for what you understand. I mean, some people need a sympathetic pat.......on the head.......with a hammer. It's not rocket science around here. It's just common sense and good food and good times. But when you throw idiots into the equation, things can get messy. Sometimes around here it seems like everyone is one window short of a view and that's just not good scenery.

Haley constantly has dramatic spells and catches diarrhea of the mouth. I have to stick my hand out and say. "Kill yourself." Jokingly of course. Sometimes Haley really gets that mouth a running with nothing in particular intelligent coming out of it. She really won't stop. "But, Missy you're not listening to me."

"Haley, I'm listening. It just takes me a minute to process the shit coming from your mouth. Can you just pretend you have stitches?"

"What is that suppose to mean?"

"Nothing Haley, It's just that I love that sound you make when you shut up. It's so peaceful."

"Missy, Why?"

"Haley cook some fries already."

Sometimes it is truly impossible to find her shut up button. She walked in to work one day. James and Kristen was sitting at the bar. She went straight for the A1 box. She opened the brand new box of A1, then looked at Kristen. "What do I do with them? Should I fill them up?"

Kristen looks over at James. "The hamster is dead again..."

One other time it was just James sitting at end of bar when she walked in.

"Missy what do I need to do?"

I looked at James as he was starting to snicker. "There really is nothing in there." Then I turned to Haley. "You're kidding right?"

192

James shaking his head. "Come on Missy, be nice. She just started." Then we both busted out.

I rubbed her face. "You're so pretty."

Keep in mind readers, she didn't just start.

Even Logan, Mr. Bubbles, has had his idiot moment around here. Especially when my Mom convinced him that the grease out of the grease trap was pudding. When he took a bite, he jumped right up from the bar stool and started to gag. "Marceline! What the hell!" Mom started laughing her ass off. "Logan, you're a little bit like a night light. It helps you find your way to the bathroom, but it's not very bright."

He cleared his throat and took a deep breath. "Sheeewwlll. Why are you always picking on me?"

"Cause I can." she said, as she walked off into the kitchen.

Ready for a couple quotes anyone?

"Common sense is a flower that doesn't grow in everyone's garden." -statusshuffle.com—

"Everyone is a genius. So if you judge a fish only on his ability to climb a tree, it will live its whole life believing it's stupid.-- 'A Einstein'

I agree with Albert, everyone does have their own niche in society. But that's not what we are talking about here people. We are talking simple everyday stuff. Not rocket science. I'm not expecting someone to do something unreasonable. We are not building cargo ships. We are cooking and serving food. All I expect from my workers is a smile and no back talk..... The way I like.... SIMPLE. Oh, and be funny, you need to be funny and sarcastic.

But even with everything seeming simple, we all have idiot moments. The real die hard idiots never survive here for very long anyway. Especially if they don't have a come back comment. They get shamed into leaving, when someone yells. "That dude is a couple electric poles away from having power." So around here, if you can't take the heat, get out of our kitchen and hit the road. If the newbies learn to reply to our sarcasm, with sarcasm, then they are usually a keeper. They fit right in. Cause sarcasm is the key through the door, even if you're an idiot.

"Life's hard. It's even harder when you're stupid." --*John Wayne*-

BEEF...... It's not just what's for dinner

So on to another type of Cafe story. It was a hot August afternoon. You could smell the garbage cooking in the dumpster. Something was gonna be fishy about today. The Cafe was about to open and people were starting to roll in. It was so hot in the Cafe, that people were sweating in their food. But, it made for a damn good night for beer sales.

As the night went on and the full moon began to rise over the knobs, you could feel trouble brewing. The coyotes began to chase their prey through the woods behind the Cafe. You could actually here their horrific howling and barking through the walls. Haley eyes were as big as bowling ball as she was waving her arm. "Oh my

God, do you guys here that? Listen ya'll, Hurry, come on, come on."
Everyone went rushing to the back door to hear what was going on.

Haley threw open the back door. "Missy you better not send me over to the garage to get cheese sticks, cause I'm not going. That is too fucking scary."

I stepped out the back door. "I know, right? One time, when Summer was about eight, I told her to come to the door and listen. The coyotes were on the hunt and had something cornered in the trees below. She asked, "Mommy, what is that? It's scary sounding." I said to her, "It's scary huh?" and she said "Yes, Mommy it is." as I leaned over to her and said, "So now, you know not to ever try to run away at night. Right?"

Haley leaned back with laughter and grabbed her chest. "Missy did you really say that to her?"

"Of course I did. She never ran away did she?"

"You're terrible, but I love ya."

I put my hand on her shoulder. "I know, but funny, right?"

I started clapping my hands. "Okay, back to work everyone. It's gonna get busy, lets keep this show on the road. Hope the coyotes don't grab any customers on their way out."

We were running around, bumping into each other like contact football. We had to be sharing each other's sweat by the end of the night. It was our usual weekend chaos, but organized chaos.

"Let's move it, let's get some food out of this kitchen. I'm ready to be done with this hot ass night."

We were knocking it out, one ticket at a time. As I was grabbing something from the end of the station, I heard a ruckus in the dish room. So I ran back and when I turned the corner, Nikki had my dishwasher up in the air, against the wall choking her. I mean, that bitch was all up in her gnats.

195

I screamed out, "What the fuck!" I grabbed Nikki and started to struggle with her. "What in Sam hell is going on?"

Another guy had to jump in to pull her off. When he stepped away, Nikki was trembling from anger and was shouting, "She has been pushing my buttons all night and when I walked by, she sprayed me with the water spigot and I snapped."

The dishwasher turned to me with a smirk on her face. "I thought she just needed a little cooling off."

I rolled my eyes. "What is wrong with you ladies?"

Nikki stuck her finger in the dishwashers face. "You must have forgot to take your meds. That was some serious unnecessary splashing."

I threw my hands up in the air. "You're kidding me right now? That's just a stupid ass reason to choke someone. Just get your salty ass back out front and take care of your tables."

Of course everyone was whispering around. "Omg, omg, omg! She was really choking her."

I was getting really aggravated. "Girls really! Let it go." I looked at the dishwasher. "Have you had a bad day? Have you both lost your marbles? You okay?"

She looked at me with a unconcerned smile. "Yep, you can't get this old woman down."

I looked at her and winked. "Girl, I don't know what that ordeal was about, but don't let anyone push you around, unless you're in a wagon or a sled. Cause that shit is fun."

Although these bitches are animated, there is nothing animated about this story. I just call it like it like I see it. Chill out ladies, I'm not calling any of you a bitch, just a figure of speech. Don't come into work after reading this, ready to tear my head off and feed it to the coyotes. You bunch of no good readers.

So, I thought that was the end of that and it was, but a new set of fools came to the forefront. It wasn't but a couple hours later when I heard Amy screaming in her deep raspy voice. It didn't strike me as unusual, but this time she was really flying off the handle. "YOU GOT SOME BEEF WITH ME?"

I heard the other waitress screaming out loud. "Fuck you Amy, just fuck you." She was holding one hand up in the air. "I only need one finger to describe how I feel about you."

Amy looked at me with red in her eyes. "I'm gonna bust her head, if she doesn't shut her fucking mouth."

With complete surprise, my voice raised above the chaos. "You need to watch your mouth." Then I motioned with my hand. "You just need to simplify this situation and go ahead and leave. I ain't dealing with this shit right now. I'm already spent just dealing with the other situation."

Amy threw her arms up. "Fine!" Then she ran toward the door in her daisy dukes. She slammed it with her kicking rocks attitude as things fell off the wall. Were customers looking? Why yes they were. The other waitress went out right behind her. I was in disbelief and mumbled to myself. "What the fuck? What is she doing? This is beyond belief." I pitched my bowl of meat down and had to leave my grill unattended, which never happens. I was pissed and about to blow a fuse. My heart was thumping. "These bitches are crazy!" I screamed as I ran toward the door.

When I got out side, with tongs in hand. The waitress was pecking on Amy's window. She was still giving her the finger, taunting her. "Fuck you Amy! Fuck you!"

Amy pushed open the door and came busting out with a beer bottle in hand. She slammed it up against the rocks, breaking off the end. The moment was becoming way to intense for me.

I screamed out, "Amy! You better put that shit down, right now!" I was waving my tong's like a weapon in the air. Which mind you would have been useless as tits on a boar hog if she had come at me.

By this time, you could feel Amy's fury. "Well.. Well.. she ain't gonna call me no bitch and get away with it. She ain't gonna follow me out to my car and keep saying fuck you.. fuck you...."

"Put it down! You two are fucking crazy" Then I pointed to the waitress. "You! Get your ass back in there!" I believe my body temperature had hit an all time high. I could have boiled some crawfish with my sweat at this point. "Amy you leave, before I have to mosquito both of your asses. Please don't make me call the law."

Amy jumped back in her car and sped off throwing rocks everywhere.

I could see that the waitress was still up in arms. "Missy, I ain't gonna work with that crazy bitch."

I put my arm around her to calm her. "Please just get back inside. Come on, we still got customers to feed." I was pleading with her to end this bullshit.

As she was trying to catch her breath, she was still fuming like a 1960 oil burning Volkswagen. "I'm telling you Missy, you need to fire her or I'm gonna have to quit."

"You don't have to do that. You know everything will be fine next week."

198

"Not this time Missy. She has gone too far, just way too far this time. I never freak out like that. She has done flipped my lid."

"I don't know the whole story." I said.

"You don't? You should, you know who I was dealing with." She said.

"It was Amy, I agree." I was trying to agree with her so she would get her ass back inside to work. We all know I didn't have the whole story. But Amy does have a tendency to stir things up. It's just in her blood.

Of course things went back to normal the following weekend. Amy was aware she had egg on her face. She was sorry, even though I seen several stink eyes being thrown around the room. Usually half way through the night, I have to tell her bi-polar ass to just go outside to her car and fire one up. She gets pissed when I say that, but I know it will chill her out. You know smoking pot does that, it chills you out, and some people need chilling out. I wouldn't tell just anyone to go get stoned, but Amy, Yes I do. But that night I needed something a little stronger, maybe a horse tranquilizer or something.

I myself would never be able to function at the Cafe if I were to smoke pot. Actually I don't function at all. I tried it once years ago when I first opened. I only smoked because I thought we were done. Then some customers walked in. I ran and hid in the back room. I looked at my waitresses and said, you have to cook for them. I wasn't going to, just wasn't gonna happen. I get way to paranoid around people when I'm high. Plus, it seems like it takes me a dick year to get something done. I can't even stand to get in the shower because it feels like it takes me a week to get clean and that's just too long and I start too panic. Some of the times I don't even know what to do with myself. I ask myself, Self? Should I eat a nut? Should I take a drink? Should I stand? Sit? Watch TV or write? I got it! Go to bed. That's a good idea.

I'm actually looking forward to writing about some high times in the future. There is only a few, funny as hell few. Still wondering why it's against the law. Guess I just admitted to breaking the law several times. Please readers, don't turn me in.

For now, lets eat some more beef. Miles came in one night, looking for her coat that she had left the week before. She had previously called me on the phone and asked, "Have you seen my jacket?"

"Nope, I sure haven't."

"Well I'm gonna find out who took it."

"That's fine Miles, do it. I don't blame you. I personally don't know where it's at."

So when she arrives to work she starts asking everyone. "I wanna know who took my fucking jacket? I left it hanging right here last week."

Some answered and seemed concerned and some avoided the question all together. It made her even more suspicious and angry. "Whose little jacket is this setting over here?"

I walked over to look. "That's been setting here all week."

She held up the jacket and yelled with huffiness in her voice. "Whose jacket is this?"

"It's mine!" Haley said.

Then Miles looked over at me and it looked like she was about to blow a gasket as she whispered under her breath. "I think Haley took it. This is her jacket, I bet she has mine, that little shit!"

I kind of looked at her funny. "But Miles, she left with you last Saturday night after work.

"Well, she had a bag full of stuff."

"Well, if she did, I'm sure it was by accident. You don't need to be working yourself up."

"Well, if it was by accident. Why didn't she bring it back? She is the only one that is as small as me, and it's a North Face. Its not like I have the money to just go buy another one. I'm gonna check her car and if its fucking in there, I'm gonna fuck that little girl's world up."

"Calm down Miles." I said.

"Dude.... take some Xanax." as Steph chimes in from her peanut gallery.

"Excuse me! I'm serious. Missy, people ain't gonna take my shit!"

"Well Jess, nobody should be taking anybody's shit. Just try to remember to take your shit home with you next time. I'm sorry it disappeared, but I don't think it was purposefully taken from anyone here. But I do understand why you are upset."

"Well, we will see! I'm gonna check other people's car too, and one in particular." She said as she walked out the door.

I never found out if the jacket was recovered. Luckily that situation eventually calmed down and I haven't heard anything else of it. Things don't usually disappear around here, I mean they have, but mostly because of the chaos. I try to weed out the thieves. No one likes a thief. Even thieves don't like thieves. Hopefully no thieves working here.

There has been drama in this place since the day I opened the doors. Drama, drama, drama. I have some loud outspoken ladies, even out spoken boys sometimes, but not as much. That's why I like guys to work with me at the grill. No periods, which means less mouth, less talk back.

201

Logan

Logan, has had a few run ins himself. Keep in mind, Logan is a little flamboyant. He sticks out like a tropical flower in a field of thistles in these here parts. "Shewwwl, I can't take this. Your waitresses are killing me." He said.

"Yep! they kill me sometimes too."

"I won't do anything Missy, unless you tell me to. They're not gonna tell me what to do around here."

"Who keeps telling you what to do?" I asked.

"Joe Mack! He even came up here and cussed me out. He wanted some money out of the drawer and I said I wasn't giving it to him. I didn't know what he wanted it for. "Open the God damn register!" He yelled. GOD..... Missy, he was so mean. He got in my face and everything."

"Well, he probably just succumbed to the pressure of this place."

"Yeah, I know, it gets stressful. Oh! And that one man that got in my face that night. You know that big customer? Oh! He got right up in my face, I was so scared Missy. He put his chest up to mine. I didn't know what to do. He was just pushing me around like a little rag doll. He was complaining about the wait, and I told him you can go somewhere else if you want. Boy, Missy, you sure learn how to deal with the public around here."

"Yep, you got too." Then I paused and thought for a moment about what he said. "You told him what?"

He looked away and avoided the question, like oh shit! I'm in trouble now. Cause he knew he had slipped up by telling me that. You never tell a customer to go some where else, never!

As I winked at him and said. "Go on with your story Logan. That's fine you told a customer to leave, you're forgiven this once."

Then he turned back around. "Eeeewwww and Amy, I was never so glad to get to rub your birthday cake all over her. She went walking past me and I smeared it all down her back. It felt so good..... She gets into it with everybody, don't she Missy?"

"Yes she does, Logan"

He was seeming to get hyper as he was speaking. "I mean like the time Amy got in Joe Mack's face out on the floor. She put her finger in his face and said. "You don't know nothing about me mother fucker." out in front of customers and everything."

203

"She has a tendency to do that Logan."

"I think maybe Amy has had it out with everyone here, and here she still stands. God love her. Her and Steph, even had it out here. Aren't they suppose to be best friends or something?"

"Sure are."

"He took both his arms and made a push gesture. "She just pushed Steph into that fridge over there like it was nothing. Shewwwllll, they were fighting over a dumb table or something. She tries to say, at least I haven't had it out with any customers. I guess, I have to give her credit for that."

"Yep! We got to give her credit for that. Her heart is in the right place. She just hasn't found the right meds yet. Unlike Haley, she says she isn't crazy because she takes her medicine."

Then Logan states seriously. "I can't do any kind of drugs, legal or illegal. I would scratch my eye balls out and my privates would be gone."

I myself, haven't had any beef with customers. Well maybe one or two, but they were drunk and rude, so they don't count.

Just to let you know, I have had several screaming matches with some of my workers. You put 15 independent, hormonal women together in a high demanding stressful job, it's bound to.... get.... a little out of hand sometimes. As crazy as this may all seem, we do all get along. We sit down with each other at the end of the night and have a beer. For the most part, we laugh about it all. With the exception of Amy and the beer bottle battle. It took a little longer for that to pass and for it to be funny. But usually we're fine by the end of the night, no matter what goes down. It's like a crazy family, we fight with each other, but no outsider would get away with messing with any of us.

I still have workers that were here from when I first opened. The only reason most people have left, is because they have graduated college and have furthered their career. We have lost several that didn't belong, and we lost them quickly. These girls in here, let you know right away if you don't fit their profile.

Like Amy would say, these bitches are gonna get kilt up in here. Some new workers took it as a legitimate threat, although Amy has never killed anyone, I don't think. She has killed some cows though. As story would have it. She was driving down the road late one night when she came upon a herd of cattle. She said. "People were trying to rustle them out of the road and back into the field. I hit them so hard, they were all over the car and all over the road. I think I even knocked a couple back into the field. I killed five of them. No one would claim them because they would get in trouble for them being out there in the middle of the road like that. I was driving this guy named Swirly's car. I don't know how I drove away because that car looked like it just came out of the Demolition Derby. He couldn't turn it in on insurance, cause I was drunk. Do you know, that the owners of the cows called them people, to take the dead cows to slaughter. Then the next day I went to eat at Golden Coral and I ordered shish kebabs. All I could think about was them grinding them suckers up for us to eat. Then I about puked. Couldn't eat beef forever after that."

Keep in mind if you're not a type A personality, you will never survive this place. It's fast pace, it's demanding and it's stressful. So, type B people, do not apply. We will swarm around you like bees and give you a sting in the ass. Maybe more like a hornet or a wasp from a few.

Most of the workers that remain here work nine to five jobs. They like working here on the weekend because the money is good and deep down we all love each other no matter what. I think.

Remember back when I said maybe, I had some beef with customers? Okay, here goes. One night my waitress came up to me frustrated and said. "Forget that one order."

I looked at her in confusion. "Which order?"

As she pointed across the bar. "The couple with kids at the bar table. They are leaving, they said it had been too long and are complaining that the table next to them got their food first."

I was thinking fuck them. You wanna know why? Because I already knew their complaint was mute. She just stood there staring at me. "What do I do?"

I replied, "For starters, here is what you do. Charge them for what they already ate, then you let them leave." I decided to walk over to them and ask politely, "What's the problem?" Although I already knew. Like little shit ass babies, they pointed at the next table and said. "They got their food first."

I'm very frustrated at this point. "Yes they did. Would you like to know why? I can tell you why. They have rare steaks and two people. You have your wife and two kids. Plus, you ordered appetizers that we had to get out to you first, and your steaks were ordered well done."

The man starts to stutter. "Well... well.." He was already standing and making a scene. "We won't be back."

I replied for the first time in this manner. "And that will be just fine sir..."

Guess what??? Two weeks later they were back. What's that tell you?

There is a whole lot more beef I could talk about. I mean a lot. But enough beef, I'm stuffed. How about you? How about some dessert or maybe a cheese stick?

IS IT 'A' CHEESE STICK

It was the end of the night. Haley was filling her freezer back up for the upcoming night. She asked Clay to help her carry some bags of stuff for her. I was sitting there at the end of the bar resting my weary legs for a moment. I watched her fill his arms up with bags of chicken, fries and cheese sticks. I just happened to be watching and caught exactly what went down. She was kneeling there on the floor doing her chore in her little happy mood. Clay is standing above her with his arms full, holding the bags toward his midsection. As Haley went to grab them, I saw her expression change from smiling, to OMG! Clay's expression changed too, it went directly to a smile. Haley looked up in surprise and swallowed. "I'm so sorry!"

Then he just laughed and walked back to his station. Haley came running to the bar in tears of laughter. "Oh My God Ya'll! I just grabbed his pecker. I thought it was a cheese stick. Then I realized it was a little warm and not frozen. I didn't know what to do. I wanted to say something but I was stunned. His girlfriend is back there with him, and Shit! Miss Frankie, his grandma! I'm so embarrassed."

I started cracking up. "Haley I don't think Miss Frankie seen it."

Haley's face was three shades of red. "I hope not. I hope she doesn't think I'm grabbing her grandson's pecker."

While at the same time this conversation was going on. Nikki was standing at the deep fryer fixing herself some cheese sticks. She pulled one out of the bag and it was only half the size it should be. She didn't know what had just went down yet. Then Clay just happened to walk past. She held up her pinky and said. "This cheese stick is that small." What's the odds? He wasn't smiling anymore. He thought she was making fun of his pecker. Which she wasn't, cause Haley had already whispered to me. It's kinda big.

Frankie responds to Nikki. "That is a small cheese stick." She didn't know what had happened either. It started to sound like to Clay, that even his grandmother was making fun of his pecker. The whole conversation went into a frenzy for a moment. With disbelief he said. "Grand-ma! I can't believe you are talking about this."

Frankie replied as her voice got loud. "Talking about what?"

Nikki replied. "The cheese stick, look! It is about the size of my pinky."

I'm about to fall out of my seat at this point. "That's a pretty small cheese stick."

Clay was getting more and more embarrassed by the moment. He was also getting frustrated by the time Haley had filled Nikki and everyone else in on what was going on. We were laughing so hard, we were about to piss our pants. Clay still thought they were talking about him and walked out the door. I'm not sure if we ever cleared up that situation with him or not. Maybe we just pulled a Beverly on him and let him go on thinking we all thought he had a pecker the size of half a cheese stick.

Short story: *Toward the end of the night, none of the girls ever want to take the last tables that come in. They always wanna come make their money and then be done. This guy came in and one of my workers didn't want to wait on him. She asked another waitress if she would take the table. "Please, Take the table, I had sex with him."*

As the other waitress replied, "Did he f*** you in the ass?" With surprise she answered. "No!"

The other waitress laughed and smacked her on the shoulder. "Well you're good then, take the table." then walked off.

So we're finished with cafe stories for the moment. I have plenty more coming at you live, from Raywick Kentucky. For now, we're gonna move along.

Yo! This is an Update.. This shit just happened. I CLOSED THE CAFE. Temporarily of course, but who knows what the future will bring. All I know is that I've been thinking about it for a minute, especially after I got broken into back in January. But let me tell you about the straw that broke the camels back. I walked into the Cafe and mom was bitching once again about the waitresses not filling up their salt and pepper shakers. I looked at her with frustration. "Really! Are they all empty?" She held them up and they were empty. "Yep! I'm closing." Now readers, know that's not what really did it. There is plenty more, like I said. IT'S THE STRAW.

JUSTICE FOR TRISH/ IT'S JUST A THING

Kathleen and Trish

Back about five years before I opened the Cafe, some serious shit went down in this town on my pawpaw's farm, and it wasn't me left on the farm to pick up walnuts. It was an unexpected twist in my families day that turned into an apocalyptic nightmare. It was March 27, 1995. I will try to explain this tragic day the best I can. Although I hate even bringing the story back to light, because it broke all the family's hearts, but the story must be told of one so fabulous.

Just hours before the call. I had just taken Summer with me to visit my aunt Trish. She lived on the Bickett farm and the road to it was connected to Raywicks one and only main highway. She lived near the back part of the farm on top of a hill in a white house. Summer was around two and a half at the time and I was twenty seven. We had just had dinner with Trish and Uncle Rick. They didn't have any kids, the dogs were their babies. While standing in her kitchen, Summer was in the other room playing with the dogs and Rick. Trish was enthralled with how well behaved Summer was. She said she never had kids because they can be little brats and we started to laugh. She looked at me and asked. Why isn't Summer a little brat. She is so lovable and sweet. So I was explaining to her what tactic I used to make Summer such a well behaved child in one long word. "OOMPA LOOMPA'S."

"OOMPA LOOMPA'S."

Trish wanted to show me some old Coke Cola stuff she had recently bought at a yard sale. She knew I was a huge cola collector. My back room of the house was completely filled with it at the time. There was this one piece that I just absolutely loved. She didn't want to give it up, but being one of the coolest Aunt's ever, she gave it to me to take home. It hangs in my Cafe today, and I'm thankful everyday that's where I put it. I moved all my cola stuff from the house when I remodeled. If I had not, I wouldn't have one thing of hers left, due to my fire! THAT HAPPENED HALLOWEEN DAY. Anybody see anything peculiar with that?

Summer.

This is how I recall the rest of the day. A couple hours after I got home, I received the unexpected phone call. "Missy, Missy, Oh dear Jesus, get to Trish's house quick!! Her house is on fire!" I don't even remember who was on the other end of the phone and I'm not going to pretend I do. All I know is that I jumped in my car and tore out of here faster than the North American X-15 rocket and headed aggressively back to the farm. As I was rolling down the curvy, one lane farm road, I about hit Charlie head on, as we both swerved and slid off to the side of the road. I threw it in reverse as my tires spun in the dirt. I rolled down the window. He yelled from his window, "Trish?"

I was confused. "Huh! It's me, Missy."

"Shit, I thought you was Trish. Have you seen her? Her GD house is on fire and we are trying to find her."

"I just seen her a couple hours ago Charlie. What the hell?" Then I sped off quickly as my tires spun out again. It was only around seven, eight or nine, o'clock I'm not sure, but it was just beginning to get dark. I thought to myself, hopefully there is no way they are in the house. As I was getting closer I could see the flames and the smoke rolling through the dusky sky. I pulled up and jumped out of my car like a mad woman. My stomach was in a ball of motion as I ran over to the front yard where everyone was gathered. My grandfather was holding my grandmother back as she screamed hysterically and desperately trying to get into the house.

I had to take a deep breath. "Holy shit! What is going on? Where is Trish? I was just here a couple hours ago."

Everyone was screaming and desperately wanting to get in the house, but the blaze was too hot. All we could do was watch, hold Grandma back, and wonder in horror. Some of the family kept saying there is no way they are in there. They wouldn't be asleep this

214

early. They would have known if something was burning. But both of their cars were sitting in the drive and that's why everyone was freaking out.

"But where are they?" Everyone was asking. Then someone said in an inspiring voice. "Maybe they went fishing. They could be out on a romantic walk or anything. They have to be around here somewhere."

The flames were getting bigger and bigger. The blaze was lighting up the sky and glaring off every ones face. By the time the fire trucks finally rolled in, the house was nearly gone.

My grandma was still screaming. "Oh my heavens! Somebody, please find my baby!"

You could tell her knees were about to give out as she continued to plea. "Please! Please! Lord heaven above, somebody find Trish now. Oooooh my baby, my baby!!!!! Oh dear Lord where is she?" As tears were flying out of her eyes. It was a sight I could hardly bare to see.

We stood there in terror and it was pure mayhem. Everyone was trying to calm each other down. My eyes were shocked with the sight of the house an how it had basically disappeared in front of me. It all seemed to happen so quickly, that I still struggle with trying to pull specific detail from it. Tears and screams were still coming from Grandma, there was no end to it. My mom looked at me. "You know they're not in there, I wish Momma would just calm down." Then Mom looked around. "Somebody take Momma to the house! Get her home, get her home now." Then she put her arms around Grandma. "Mom! They're not in there. Let us take you home and wait for Trish. They're just out on the farm somewhere, probably picking you up a gallon of walnuts or something."

"Ooohhhh Marceline!! Please tell me she is not in there."

215

"She isn't Mom. Please let me take you home."

"But Marceline! Why wouldn't they see the flames and come running?"

"I don't know Momma, maybe they're down in the holler."

"But why wouldn't they hear the fire trucks?"

By this time the investigators were asking us all to leave, but we were still waiting for Trish and Rick to show up. They said there is nothing you can do here. So they packed Grandma up in the car with her fighting us every step of the way. As Paw-paw drove off, she stared out the window, hesitant to leave. We were all still hoping for good news as we all continued to follow, one by one.

Someone had already called my Grandma's, brothers and sisters who lived a couple towns over. They were standing outside at Grandma's house when I pulled up.

I heard them yelling as their faces were lighting up. "Trish is here! Trish is here! She just pulled in, we found her!" My heart was lifted, but just for a blink of an eye. As I was looking all around to see where she was, there was no Trish in sight. Have they gotten confused? Then....I realized, I was the only one who had pulled in. They had already taken off, running toward the house, to get Grandma, before I could even get out of the car.

They were yelling with excitement, from the screen porch, for Grandma to come outside. "Trish is outside!!!! She just pulled in. Come on Coletta,"

I can honestly say that I have never felt like I wanted to be someone else so much in all my life. I was standing there stiff as a board when Grandma came running out of the house looking desperately all around.

"Where? Where?" She was excessively affected by emotions.

"Oh Lord, Coletta!" With a voice of despair, their eyes dropped to the ground.

The look and disappointment on my grandma's face was unforgettable when she realized I wasn't Trish. "That's Missy, you fools." Her sister's faces turned somber, after they realized what they had implied. This followed with another total breakdown of my Grandma. It broke my heart in so many places. I was so sick I couldn't even speak, all I could do was hang my head. Thinking, Trish! Please! Be somewhere, please God! Let her and Rick be somewhere other than in that house.

Everyone was pulling in at Grandmas, full of fear and questions. Where could they possibly be? They couldn't have been at home. That just doesn't make any sense, and if they weren't at home. How did the house catch a fire?

"Maybe it's the land," someone said. "Joe Keith's house burnt down on that same spot back in the eighties."

Before anyone could answer, the phone rang. Please let it be Trish I thought. My grandma franticly picked up the phone. Whomever was on the other end of the line, relayed a horrifying message that, YES! IN FACT, THEY WERE IN THE HOUSE.

It had to be the most chilling call a parent could ever receive. No one ever expects to lose their child this way. I had never seen my Grandma lose it like she did at that moment, even more so than at Trish's house, at least she had hope. Now all hope was lost and she just about fainted. We all had experienced death before, but this was the worst. How could one death be worse than the other? I don't know. It just was, and it got even worse.

I stood there dumbfounded and mute. Emotion swept over my body, and I myself felt faint. My mind simply wouldn't compute. I was desperately trying to keep up with the information that was being handed to us after two beautiful people had just been stolen from all of us. Was it an accident or something more sinister?

The sad thing is, my memory couldn't even tell you how my own child ended up with her dad. My mind was a wreck. I don't recall him getting her or if I even had her at the time. I mean I couldn't have had her with me. I recall driving straight there, or did I? Maybe I drove her to her dads first. It was all so crazy, and it continued to get crazier.

Everyone was so grief stricken and in shock. My grandma was so bad that Charlie had to call the doctor, and we basically had to tranquilize her with pills. My grandmother wasn't known to take pills, only her daily vitamins. We were all there, can't name us all. Everyone but Joe Keith and Jimmy, who were still in prison without a clue of what had happened to their beloved little sister. Their sister whom would never see her dreams fulfilled. A sister they would never get to hug again.

The next day, we were alarmed with new information. It was definitely an unexpected twist and development. We got the news from the coroner and they had determined that they had been shot. YES! SHOT! Two innocent lives snuffed. We now had two shocks to absorb.

This sent the family into complete panic. We could not believe what we were hearing. What really happened? As the neighbors were told of the murders, they were both devastated and terrified. Everyone was wondering who would want to kill two such beautiful people. The news cameras were in town interviewing people. Many were in fear that there was someone killing couples. Questions were plaguing the whole town. It made the entire community feel vulnerable. Was it a neighbor or a stranger? Who knew? No one knew. Oh my God, shot! Who would shoot them? Who in this town would shoot them? We all had been in and out of that road that day. Holy crap, he could have gotten all of us. How did we not see someone drive in? How did this mystery person elude us? The answer was going to require a deeper look.

I heard Charlie ask, "Missy, wasn't you just up there?"

"I was."

Then Mom looked at Charlie agitated. "How did you not notice anyone Charlie? You live right across the field?"

"I don't know Marceline. Daddy was on the farm too, all day long bulldozing."

We just couldn't figure it out. Not only were we experiencing and mourning the loss of Trish and Rick, the hunt for a murderer had begun. More questions begin to be asked. There was a murderer among us. We all feared for our safety. No one could have predicted what had really happened and what had been done to our Trish

That night, we flocked together like sheep. Half of my cousins stayed at my house. We were scattered all over the floor. We stayed up most of the night, truly and totally afraid. Trying to figure out what the hell was going on.

I myself was still in nursing school at the time and was supposed to be there the next morning.

So when we awoke I rolled over and pecked Kristen on the shoulder. "I've got to quit, I've got to go there and quit. Kristen! Will you please get up and ride with me?" So we got up, walked across everyone sleeping in the floor, and took off. I don't know why I felt like I had to take care of it that instant, but only maybe, to get away from the madness that I was struggling to deal with. When I got there I explained the situation to my teacher. She told me to take a little time off. I didn't have to quit. She would work it out for me.

When we got home, I went back down Grandmas. They were already planning funeral arrangements. Wait a minute! This is all happening so fast. What has just happened? Why were they shot? Who killed them? And why burn the house down?

As I walked into the kitchen, I spotted the pill bottle that the doctor had sent down to my Grandma. This would be my first encounter with valium. I took a hand full and started handing them out to my cousins, the ones of age of course. I have to say, It had a very calming effect. I went from feeling like I was having a nervous breakdown, to a calm steady illness like nausea. I was calm as a lamb going to slaughter, but in a cloud of dust.

I had heard later that day, that my uncle Louis Earl actually stayed at the house with the detectives when they went in to recover and identify the bodies. I can't imagine the vision that would be stuck in his head for the rest of his life, to see your sister burnt beyond recognition. Till this day, I don't know what made him walk in there. It would be horrifying to the mind and a lasting haunting memory. It was disturbing enough just reading the files. I can't imagine the actual image. I had trouble in nursing school during my clinicals, just seeing strangers in pain, dying or an actual body. That shit just can't be unseen.

Tessa, Joe Keith, Grandma, Trish and Jimmy.

We sent for a request to let the boys come home from prison so they could attend the burial and bereavement. But the police tried to accuse Trish and Rick of being part of the drug deals that had gone on in recent years. They tried to claim that Trish and Rick worked the other end of the drug deals down in Florida and helped traffic it. They were barking up the wrong tree and it was complete bologna and an outrageous assumption. The boys couldn't come home. It added insult to injury. This had to break their hearts on every level. I just couldn't imagine. So we had to go forward with the burial plans, and it double broke my Grandma's heart knowing her boys couldn't come home just for this. Did they think they were gonna sell pot at the funeral. Trust me, we all could have used some.

While at the funeral home we were sitting in the break room. Someone had slipped Beverly a pill to calm her down. Must have been a really strong one. She went from trembling to giddy as hell and was making some kind of crazy jokes. The guests heard us laughing all the way out in the arrangement room. We almost had to put our hands over her mouth. That pill had made her loose some of her marbles. We all had at the moment, we were at our breaking point. Obviously that pill pulled out her humor for the moment. A brief moment.

An overflow of people attended the funeral. It was a God awful experience and I need not get into all the detail about it, just know the funeral was sad.. sad... sad, just as any funeral would be, except with detectives and not all the family.

As we sat and listened to the eulogy, the priest talked about Trish and Rick and how they got married on Valentine day back in 1982 at Saint Thomas, in the Virgin Islands. He stated that Trish was a part time model for Drakes Casual Wear and Rick was an electrical engineer. They made their home in Tampa Florida after Rick finished his job there. Their honeymoon trip was taken to the British Island, Nevis. Trish was loving life and living it well. All she had left to do was come home to her mom and dad.

At times during his speech, I was crying so hard, I couldn't see through my tears.

Trish had just moved back from Florida just a few years prior to this tragedy. She wanted to come back to Kentucky, because family was very important to her. Even though she and Rick had a very good life and good jobs in Florida, she missed her mom the most. Now we all miss her. She was a ray of sunshine and full of life and energy. Her life was horrifically cut short at the age of thirty-eight. Rick was a bit older than Trish. He was fifty-one at that time.

Trish was petite and adorable and had a heart of gold. She had a beaming personality and reminded me of a fairy or a sweet little pixie of some sort. She would swoop into your home and make the sun shine, fart out fairy dust on you from head toe. Then poop a few rainbows on the way out. That's just who she was. People said we looked a lot alike. That must have been the reason for everyone's confusion. but I don't carry the complete and utter charm she had, not to say that I can't be charming at times.

"All the world is made of faith, and trust, and pixie dust" J.M. Barrie

One of Summer's sketches. Reminded me of Trish.

After the funeral and the bereavement, the whole family was still in fear of who, and why, someone had committed this heinous crime. The newspaper head lines read, 'RAYWICK COUPLE MURDERED, HOUSE BURNED. It was all over the news, statewide. Police were searching high and low.

Trish had been shot twice in the face and her husband Rick, had been shot twice in the head, basically execution style. They were found in separate rooms and their bodies burned beyond recognition. Trish's two dogs were found dead lying in her arms near the back door, obviously trying to escape the man's madness. But maybe not. Since she was shot in the face, maybe she was entering the back door as he ambushed her. Maybe she could have been taking him on while fighting for her life. We will never know.

I don't recall the police ever talking to me. You would have thought they would, since they usually talk to the family first. They investigate every angle from the inside out. I guess they already had a suspect.

A few days later the police arrested a man, of no name to me. Not just a man, a psychotic man, whose name I won't ever mention, EVER. They charged him with two counts of first-degree murder and first-degree arson.

We wanted justice for Trish, but with the boys in jail, was it gonna be enough. Every one in the family was feeling numb. I was numb. Sometimes words not even spoken. Why? We had lost our beloved Trish. Completely out of natural order and in such an inhuman way, we had no words to say. I cant imagine the pain my Grandma felt, losing her child in such a horrific manner. How do you hold on to hope?

A bass boat was recovered at the fucker's house, among other evidence, including a .22-caliber magnum revolver. It has been said that he had given my uncle a cold check. Rick just wanted him to make good on his money, but he did not. So Rick went and took the boat back, which anyone would have done. That no name son-of-a-bitch, drove back up to the farm. Down our one lane road in the broad open daylight, armed with a gun, a gas tank and a boat hitch. He shot my aunt and uncle in cold blood, torched their house, and had the nerve to hook up to the boat and haul it back to his house. What the hell? He obviously was harboring some intense rage and psychosis. To kill for such a trivial reason and disregard to human life, that no rational person would ever imagine doing. It was just cruel and made no sense. I won't go into details about the trial, there really wasn't one. The case was settled quickly because he pled out. Case closed. His excuse was that he got angry, which is no freaking excuse at all. He went into their home, preying on the innocent like hornets devouring a bee hive, with no guilt what so ever.

I could drag this story out across the whole damn book, but I just can't and won't bring myself to do it. It is too heartbreaking. I just cant imagine what Trish went through in her last moments. Especially after reading part of the autopsy report stating she had smoke in her lungs, which means she possibly could have still been alive for a bit. After reading that, my stomach went ill and I had to shut the files and ask the lady to file it back away. I didn't need to know more. I already knew enough. It made me feel so disturbed in a way I was unfamiliar with. I can't imagine what parents go through, when they have to relive the event, when they put these stories on *Dateline* or *Forensic Files.*

Quote: *"There comes a time when all of us are dead. All of us. There will come a time when there are no human beings remaining to remember that anyone ever existed or that our species ever did anything. There will be no one left to remember Aristotle or Cleopatra, let alone you. Everything that we did and built and wrote and thought and discovered will be forgotten' and all of this will be for naught, Maybe, that time is coming soon and maybe its a million years away, but even if we survive the collapse of our sun, we will not survive forever. There was time before organisms experienced consciousness, and there will be time after. and if the inevitability of human oblivion worries you, I encourage you to ignore it. God know that's what everyone else does."* ---John Green, *The fault in Our Stars.*-

I NEED NOT SAY, YOU SHOULD KNOW.

Starting from left, you have Joe Keith, his son Jamie, then Jimmy and the infamous Johnny Boone, Beverly, I don't know, and Robbie, at the penitentiary.

The irony to the story is a sad one also. In 1990 Trish had written many letters to the Kentucky House of Representatives, speaking of the drug control act. She wasn't aware of this law until her two brothers were charged with conspiracy to distribute marijuana. Then they received 20-25 years without parole. Which is bullshit. Why? Because the boys were subjected to a mis-justice. I just watched a case on television the other night where a man had slit his brothers throat. He received seven years. They let him out in two! Only to murder, rape, and beat a woman. Then attacked and almost killed a female state trooper. How in the hell does one get a chance to murder again? What is wrong with our system? Trish was obsessed with trying to help her brothers get less time for a non violent crime, pretty much a victimless crime.

She stated in her letter: *That incarcerating a man that long, with no violence involved, is totally unreasonable. I thought our prison was to rehabilitate, not stick someone in prison only to become bitter. Even murderers get parole. I ask myself, If I had a daughter and she was raped by a man, or if she had a man to ask her if she wanted to buy some marijuana, who would I hate the most? Who would I want to spend life in prison? I need not say, you should know.*

The man, if you wanna call him that. The one whom murdered Trish and Rick, received life in prison. Guess what? He has the possibility of a parole hearing in 2021? Something my uncles didn't get, a parole hearing. This man could be out walking the streets in my lifetime. I do believe Trish would maybe roll over in her grave if she knew our justice system was still that messed up. The fact that people are spending more time in prison for marijuana, than people with violent crimes is just absurd. VIOLENT CRIMES! LIKE 'A' DOUBLE HOMICIDE. YES! I'M YELLING AGAIN.

Back when it all happened, my Grandma felt empathy for the man's family; she stated to the papers; "Its more than what some could do, but they had no control over his actions. A man commits his own crime, and it is bad when that family has to suffer too. It's not good for anyone."

229

---WE ARE EACH OUR OWN DEVIL AND WE MAKE THIS
WORLD OUR OWN HELL-- (OSCAR WILDE)

With that quote being said and as true as it could be. Just know that in this Maniacs case, he made many peoples lives hell. So just know that other people can do it for you. You're not always in control of your own destiny. I believe everyone is capable of sin, but to me, all sins aren't forgivable. This sure in the hell is one of them. They say, let he who have not sinned, cast the first stone. Well, lets just say, I would throw the whole f**kin rock quarry at him.

My grandma is against the death penalty and so was my Pawpaw, even though he still thought the man deserved it. He stated to the local paper the reason he would like to see the death penalty. It was only because of all the leniency he has seen on violent crimes. My Pawpaw said It's just not fair to have two sons in prison and to see this man receive the same sentence. It would be just another devastation.

Mr and Mrs. J.E. Bickett, AKA Grandma and Paw-paw

I would like to make a quick note of what my Grandma stated to the papers at the time...

"I know the Bible says an eye for an eye, but I'm not that blind yet. I've always been against the death penalty and that's up to God. You can't say the 'Our Father' unless you can forgive people. On the morning after Trish's death, "It seemed like the end of the world, but after a strong sedative, I seemed to relax. I kept thinking that maybe God had plans for her. Then I would ask God, why did you permit this to happen? I was feeling so mixed up. I kept thinking that if I didn't think about it, it would just go away, like a bad dream, and she would come back to me. I knew in my heart she was safe in heaven, and had achieved what we all were striving for, eternal life. But knowing this, did not ease my pain. I even resented God and his ability to give and take life. I now realize just how fragile life is... But it's such a shock when death comes to someone we love more than we love ourselves..."

My aunt Trish didn't have to have a special occasion to stop by except to say she loves us and to bring my Grandma flowers, yellow roses usually. She joked and made us laugh and her attitude was infectious. She would go out of her way to do anything for anyone. She was young, vibrant and happy, with lots of life to live. I'm not just saying this because she has passed, I'm saying this because it is true. It's hard to come across unselfish people like her. I swear I never heard her say a cross word to anyone.

Trish's death put a very black cloud on the whole family for a long time. My grandma being affected the most. I'm sure she was simmering with resentment, which I totally understand. Who wouldn't? I feel that she has never fully recovered from this horrifying event. Something inside her died along with Trish that day. She often spills out bitter words from all her pain and that is understandable too. Even though nothing ever really went back to normal for Grandma, she has held on to her wit and her story telling. Although the family at some point, somehow, emerged from the pain and grief. But no one was left unmarked by this terrible, terrible inexcusable incident.

We all at sometime in our life have to learn to get use to and learn a new way of living after we have lost someone so close in our lives. It's one of the highest obstacles we have to cross. We all miss Trish and speak of her constantly. She was the mediator, the glue of the family, which kept us bonded. After her death my mom, kinda stepped into her shoes, to try and hold the family together in that trying time.. But mind you, no one could be our special Trish, she was a NATURAL at being happy and making people feel happy too.

I pray to God that somehow the message Trish was trying to point out, doesn't keep falling on deaf ears in our government. Especially the lawmakers, the ones who seem more concerned with arresting someone for rolling a joint than someone who beats someone to death. Quit wasting your time hovering over our town with your damn dope choppers. Why not try to spend our tax dollars on catching the real criminals, like people in slave trade and sorts. None of this feels quite like justice.

I guess this incident makes me question destiny, miracles and life itself. How would this be anyone's destiny? The truth of the matter, its not, it's life. We are all born with a death sentence.

Quotes that Trish seemed to lived by: And would want us to do the same:

"You cannot control what happens to you, but you can control your attitude toward what happens to you and in it, you will be mastering change rather than allowing it to master you." ---Brian Tracy----

One of the simplest ways to be happy is... letting go of the things that make you sad.----daily dose----

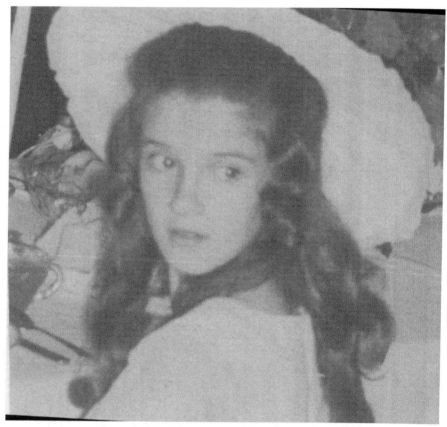

Kathleen's wedding

REMEMBER HER FOR HER.

Everything about this story hurts, but now I want to remember her for her. Not how she died, but the joy she brought to us while she was here.

I wanted to know more about Trish in her younger years. I only knew of the few things I've told you. Like the time she had pulled out most of my hair with a hair dryer and made me look like a little pygmy. I knew she loved to dance and sing, because its in her genes.

Plus, we both moved away at some point. I remember when she lived in Louisville. I was younger then and have no details, except that she let me ride her horses. During the few years she was here, she helped the boys, Robbie and Charlie run the new Bickett's bar.

That was after Pawpaw's original Squires Tavern burnt down. Burned down! Yes! It was torched. There all kinds of rumors, but we won't get into that at the moment.

I was really searching for some crazy funny stories to tell. So I asked Mom, to tell me about Trish when she was younger. This is what Mom had to say:

"Well Missy, I was quite a bit older than Trish, about nine years I reckon'. I married your dad when she was around nine or ten. Mom and Dad were more liberal with her and Robbie, than they were with any of us other brothers and sisters. When we had the time we always treated her like a little princess, just like a little angel. We would even give her the fudge bowl to lick, even though the rest of us wanted it. I didn't have much time to play with her because it was school, then chores, then to the upstairs to stare out the windows." as she started to laugh.

"Yep, I remember those windows." I said.

She starts getting antsy in her seat. "I just wanna get this in. This isn't about Trish. I wanna tell you a story about Beverly real quick."

"Mom, I need a story about Trish"

She starts to pat me all over. "Hold on, let me tell you this while I'm thinking about it. I can't remember if Kathleen was with us or not. I'm almost sure she was. She would have to be. I would have to ask her. Look, we're down below the Troutman's house, in the field next door."

"I know the place, that's where I split my arm wide open." I said.

"Shuh, Missy. Look! There is a little Shetland pony down there. Beverly was such a little freakin' book worm, she never did wanna do anything with us. She tries to tell me it was because I was to bossy. She never would play hop scotch or nothing. We finally got her to go down there with us to ride this little Shetland pony. Missy,

I swear. Look hear, she was so funny, it was unreal. She gets on that Shetland pony and her legs were longer than I don't know what. They where hangin' on the ground like this. I mean real long, she had really long legs. I never will forget it. I picked up a rock, and I hit the horse. That little Shetland pony took off with her and she fell off of it. Missy, I tell you what, she broke her arm so bad."

"You threw a rock?"

"Listen, Momma was having bunco that night. It started around five o'clock. We were just supposed to go out back and play, and look! Mom didn't have bunco for years and years and years. And look here, I remember I walked up, I mean Kathleen and I walked up to Momma, look; we left Beverly there, can you believe it. You would have thought one of us would have stayed there with her. Momma was on the front porch and I said, Momma. I think Beverly is really hurt or something. Maybe you ought to walk down here, and you know what she told me. You just get back down there and play. Now this is a true story; we go back down there and then we come straight back up and said, Momma! Beverly cant get up off the ground. Her arm, oh, when they took her to the doctor, I could see the bone sticking out right now. Three different places."

"Oh my God. I bet she hates you."

"Oh her arm was AWFUL. That's why it still hurts today, I guarantee it does. Bones were STICKIN' out of her arm, you could just see the bone, it was horrible. That's why…. I'm so close to Beverly today," as she starts laughing again. "I mean I'm convinced I threw the rock, maybe, I don't know. Maybe Kathleen threw the rock."

"Maybe! The memory is crazy, isn't it? But you would think you would know who threw the rock."

238

"Well I don't. I mean Kathleen tells me stories today about us as a kid and I just don't remember some of them. Look; this little girl, not little now, she lives in Michigan. Her name was Hazel Leake. Kathleen will tell you this Missy, it's true. I only had one little friend, Kathleen had all the little girlfriends around. She wouldn't let me play with them. She said because Hazel wouldn't play with her and she played with me, she was gonna change that. So she went in HAZEL ANNS MOTHER'S house and turned the water on in the bathtub and overflowed the whole room and it started seeping out into every room. It really got Hazel in trouble. She did things like that when she was little."

"She was a conniving little shit, wasn't she?"

"Look; I will never forget, I looked in the toilet one time and Jeanette, oh Jeanette! She never would play with me either. Real smart girl, look; They were pinching each other tits, trying to squeeze milk out of their tits" as she chuckles. "Then Kathleen turned around and seen me and screamed. "Shut that door, you're not invited. You're not playing with us." I thought what in the hell are they doing, I can remember THAT very plain. But I can't really remember a lot of stories about Trish."

"Well, that sucks!"

"All I know Missy is we just took care of her when we could. You know we did a lot of work at that age. I ironed, we cooked, did the cleaning. Momma had her hands full with all of us kids. I can remember just going to confession on Saturday and saying the rosary every night before we went to bed at five o'clock." as her voice got loud and fast. "We went to school, then we went to bed. So how in the hell do you think we had time to play with her. We didn't have time to play with anybody." as she started to laugh again.

239

Side note: *We always have to keep in mind, any of us can go at anytime. So what have you done today, to leave your legacy. Trish left hers and she will never be forgotten.*

So, the other day I decided to go visit Charlie. As I was pulling in, I just about ran over three of his chickens. Then when I got out of the truck his little dog started humping my leg, as Charlie came walking out of the cabin. "What's up Melissa Carol? It seems that little one likes you."

"Hey Charlie, it does seem to have a crush on me."

"What can I do for you?"

"Well, I rode up here to see if you could tell me a delightful or funny story about Trish. You wanna share any today?"

"I. I. I. I. Gotta think, there is so many of them. Uh, uh, Trish wasn't around but so many years there. She lived in Florida most of the time."

"I'm not really wanting stories about down in Florida. Maybe when she was younger or when she came back home."

He lifts his hat and scratches his head. "I'm talking bout when we went to visit her. Give me a day, I. I. will tell you a good one."

"What about down there at the bar or something?"

He reaches and takes his cigar out of him mouth. "Well...Uh, uh You know about her death, this and that. I can tell you something that preludes that death. Uh, uh, the day that we got raided. State Police, the ABC raided us up there at the bar. So that was on a Saturday night and I was all tore up about it. Main reason is cause they was gonna close us down. That next morning, Trish and Rick, now this ain't funny though, they came to the bar there. So Trish saw me all tore up like this and that. Then uh, uh I started to tell her, you know the Fifth Wheel gets away with every GD thing around here

240

and you know what she said? Charlie, it's just a thing. Don't worry about it, it's just a thing honey. She said, we'll talk about it when I get back from Lowes. She asked me if I wanted anything and gave me a great big kiss, hugged me, said I love you and don't worry about those things. And you know the next day, she is dead.

"Just a thing huh? That's the type of attitude I remember. Wish I was more like her. I try not to complain, but sometimes life just makes ya."

"Uh, uh Yes, I. I. know. But she, she told me that morning, it's just a THING. Here I was worried about getting some darn ole tickets. That's what I miss about Trish. She always kept me from worrying."

"That's all you got Charlie?"

"Oh! I do have one funny story that she told me about down there in Florida. I know you don't wanna hear about Florida, but I gotta tell you this. She said Jimmy and Angela came to visit her one time. They was setting there on the beach, and Jimmy's dick was hanging out of his pants there. Anyway, she just happened to notice it. She said she looked around there and was embarrassed for him and didn't know how to tell em. They were probably all high, this, that, and the other. She couldn't ignore it though. It was just hangin out there for the pelicans to get. So she finally looked at Jimmy, and said put your dick in your britches by God. Jimmy looked around and shuffled it a little bit. But I swear, she did tell me that one time. That was funnier than hell there. But I don't know if you can tell that kind of story there in your book, but it wouldn't hurt nothing, I don't guess. But I can't think of nothing else right off hand. I gotta sit around here and smoke a joint before I think about anything like that. Come back and see me tomorrow."

Although I haven't gotten a chance to ride back up. What I've just realized, is that maybe he was pulling my leg on the shuffle thing. Why? Because I just discovered while writing this is that he doesn't stutter as much when he tells a fib. I may have just written a fib on Jimmy. Charlie is gonna be laughing his ass off with this one. Sorry Jimmy, sure you're use to it by now and if not you should be.

My aunt Kathleen, Mom's twin whom is looking a lot like Janice
Dickerson in her modeling career days.

Let's return to the main story. Summer and I were still living in the garage after the fire. It was a couple days before Christmas in 2008. Summer and I was sitting there watching *Project Runway* when my phone rang. I was alarmed with the news that Kathleen just had an aneurysm and they were Stat Flighting her to Louisville hospital. Everyone was in a panic once again. We all knew the survival rate was low, because aneurysms are some serious shit. I was told not to rush up that night, so the next day I drove up to see what her state was. When I walked into the room, I immediately stopped at the door, I just stood there like a deer in headlights. She looked plain pitiful laying there on the bed looking lifeless. She was on a ventilator, with tubes running out from her everywhere. Her crowns had been knocked out from when they tried to resuscitate her the night before. It looked as if she had little pencil lead teeth. I tried to swallow and speak, but I couldn't. I was feeling overwhelmed and I slowly backed out of the room. I wasn't gonna be able to hold in what I was feeling. Kristen noticed my reaction and grabbed hold of me and walked me down the hallway as I began to cry. Kristen was saying, "Mom looks terrible doesn't she? I know how you feel. Let's go over here and talk, it's hard for me to stay in there and look at her." We talked for a while so I could gather myself to go back in.

The doctors were telling us she didn't have a very good chance. But what do doctors know? I only say that because, Guess what? She made it. Just to make this long, sad story short, and leave out all the heartache. I'm just gonna tell you she defied all the odds. Thank the Lord, she is still with us, after a long extensive stay in the hospital, but she is alive and kicking.

It was really a couple months of struggles and worries and uphill battles. She finally got out on February 14, 2009. Her demeanor had

244

been change by the aneurysm. She looks the same, but her attitude has become untroubled and tranquil. It seems now that she is wandering around in the sixties with her carefree attitude. She seems to never be in a hurry or concerned with a thing, maybe what someone would act like after taking a handful of Xanax. It wouldn't matter if a bear jumped out at her or if she won the lottery, she would have the same reaction. I mean she kind of had the same attitude before, but it is definitely enhanced. Sometimes when she talks, happy or sad, right or wrong, know it or not know it, she sounds the same. Her and Mom have always done crazy things, off the wall things, that will keep you in stitches. They actually try to out do each other with their craziness and desire to get attention. Example anyone? We were sitting and watching a basketball game at a restaurant. Kathleen knows nothing of sports, but just to get attention, she slowly got up from the table and raised her arms up in the air and in lackadaisical way and yelped. "Woo woo woo."

Then we were sitting at the drive thru at White Castle, when she decided to slowly exit the car, get down on the ground and crawl around barking like a dog, not a mean crazy dog, but a Non-enthusiastic one. Crazy or not crazy, enthusiastic or not, that was some funny shit and the cheapest entertainment I've had all year. She doesn't have a care in the world and it seems to aggravate everyone around her. Mom was telling me that the other day, that Kathleen got some glass stuck in her ankle. It hit a vein and blood was squirting everywhere. Mom said, she was really worried about her. But, Kathleen didn't seemed to be concerned, even though her shoe started filling up with blood. Mom told me, Kathleen just emptied out her shoe and said whoopsie, I'm going home to take a nap.

Soon after the incident (the aneurism that is) she came over to the Cafe to have coffee with Mom and I. I asked her, what exactly

245

happened that day they flew you to Louisville? She actually responded with high spirits, but at the same time like it was no big deal. Then started to tell me the story.

"Okay, here goes, just listen for a minute." she said. "I was out in the garage right before Christmas. All of a sudden, I felt this strange feeling in my head. I thought, geez.... I never felt anything like this before. So anyhow, it kept getting a little bit stronger, and I thought this doesn't seem right. You know, it was different than a headache. So I was gonna walk in and I was gonna get Danny up from his nap. You know he has to have his naps. He is like an old grizzly bear. But anyway, I had never had a major headache prior to that. This is the first bad headache I had ever had my entire life. Really Missy, it's true. So I walk out of the garage and I'm about 50 feet from the house. So I'm thinking I will just walk up the sidewalk, go in the house, to wake my husband up. Then I nudge Danny and say, Danny.....Danny.....I think I'm having an aneurysm. I had heard people describe them, I just knew that's what it was. You know, cause I'm smart like that. Danny jumped up, like what! What! I told him that I thought I was gonna jump in the shower."

I replied. "Ha….. That's what I did, when my water broke. Guess we like to be clean when we know we are going to the hospital. That clean panty thing must have really stuck with us."

"But listen Missy, the headache was getting worse. So I thought to myself, nope! I wont do that. So, we go immediately straight to the truck. We get in the truck and headed to Lebanon. I say to Danny Cecil. Danny can you drive a little faster? And he says. Honey, I'm driving as fast as I can. There's no way he was…. I just kept saying hurry up all the way there. He is the slowest driver on God's green earth. When we got there, I stepped out of the truck and I went completely blank from there. Right there at the truck, right before going into the hospital."

I'm sitting there amazed with the quietness from Mom. You and I both know, she isn't quiet by no means.

Kathleen starts to speak again with a I survived and kicked its ass attitude. "So anyway, while in hospital they told me I wouldn't walk for six months. I walked in three days after rehab. They said I would be in a wheelchair sixth months to a year. I was never in a wheelchair, I got out of the wheelchair while in rehab."

"Well, you sure showed them," I said.

Mom responded in a low voice as tears swept her eyes. "I thought you was gonna die."

Kathleen turns around in her seat. "Oh! oh! Let me tell you a funny thing that happened while I was in the hospital. I remember I told Danny my good friend was there. They had those long pillows that you put between your legs and stuff. I looked at Danny and said, Dear Lord. Why is Carol in bed with me? She was a good friend of mine while Danny was in the service. I was wondering, why is she in bed with me. Then Danny started to talk. I was like, don't talk out loud Danny, Carol is in bed with me and she has had an aneurysm too. So don't disturb her, our heads hurt really bad. Then Danny comes up, stands by the bed and I say shhhh, she is sleeping. Then he hits the pillow real hard, I mean as hard as he can. And I go, wa-wa-wa! Why would you do that to Carol? She is a good woman. Missy I'm telling you, thing's happened like that all day long every day, due to the aneurysm you know. I was completely out of my mind."

"I bet it was crazy." I said.

Mom was still sitting there quietly with wide open ears. Which was unusual. She was letting her have the lime light. They usually try to speak over top of each other, each of them always trying to blurt out a better story. Today was your day Kathleen.

Summer with her Rock band guitar.

So it's still winter of 2008 and a new year was upon us. The house is gone, Kathleen was still in the hospital and the winter had been long and cold as a well diggers ass. Summer and I were still cramped up in that small garage. It was so small that the mice were fighting for a place to take a shit. I had just gotten Summer the game *Rock Band* for Christmas. She thought it was the best thing since sliced bread. But oh boy! It was a bad decision on my part. That whole winter Haley would come over after work and they would play it till four in the morning. Singing at the top of their lungs, while standing only feet from my bed. The worst part is that they would sing the same song over and over again. There were times where I felt like I just wanted to go outside and climb a tree.

Wanna dose? *Cause it's nine in the afternoon, and your eyes are the size of the moon. You could, cause you can so you do, we're feeling so good, just the way that we do. When it's nine in the afternoon, your eyes are the size of the moon, you could, cause you can, so you do, we're feeling so good.*

And guess what? They repeat that verse three more times. Imbedded in my head? Yep! I would say so. People asked why on earth would I let this happen, why would I let Haley and them stay up for hours on end. Well for starters, I was depressed, but not so much that I wanted my child to be. So I let them sing till the wee hours of the morning. Contrary to belief, I'm very aware of other people's feelings.

Summer was a very messy teenager. Sorry to say, she still is! When it comes to her clothes that is. They occupy the whole floor. The word closet doesn't exist in her world. They say Virgos are tidy in their head, but not with their surroundings. She was my own personal little tornado. So I had let her untidiness ride all through the winter. Stepping over her stuff, picking it up, moving it, shaking out the mice turds. No, just kidding. We didn't really have any mice at all.

But that picking up stuff came to an abrupt end one day when I walked in. She was sitting on the couch watching TV and eating popcorn. As I walked across the floor, I stepped on one of her shoes. It hurt like hell and I lost it, I mean.... I lost it. I cursed her left and right, as profanities flew out of my mouth, then I threw the shoe up against the wall. "That's it! I have had it with this bullshit." She just sat there staring at me with her judgmental eyes. "Mom! What is the big deal?" She was in complete shock. Her eyes wide open and her mouth dropped. "Have you lost your mind?"

"No! I haven't lost my damn mind! Pick up your freaking shoes and get off the damn couch."

"Why don't you just calm your titties."

"What! What did you say to me?"

"Take a chill pill, Mom."

"Summer! I've been taking chill pills. That's how this place got like this. We are gonna clean today. You hear me, we're gonna clean. This place is a pig sty."

"Fine Mom, whatever. All you had to do was ask."

She was mumbling some stuff under her breath, but I ignored it and turned on the radio and cranked it up. But before it was done, more was sung, than done. We ended up jamming to *Katy Perry's, I kissed a girl and I liked it.* We were dancing around in the floor like we were at a rave. Thank you Katy for turning our frown upside down.

Now that I look back on it. To her, I must have looked like I had lost my mind at that very moment. I'm sure she was thinking in her mind, what was the big deal? We had been living like that for months. Why would I freak out now? I guess because I had just enough. I woke up and was slipping out of my depression. I'm... Back.... In fact, I had run out of valium. Wink, Wink. I was seeing the shit around me for the first time since the fire. I had come back from the dead, or may I rephrase that and say, land of the lost. That shoe was my wake up call. Was it my destiny to step on it? Hell no! Or yet Maybe! Lets just say, it was like one of those thing you break under someone's nose to wake them up after they have been knocked completely out. I see though why she just didn't get it. I understand looking through a teenagers eye's why she wouldn't. I have the power to do that you know, remembering what its like to be a teenager. Hope you readers do too, it helps a lot when dealing with teenagers, remembering you were one yourself.

I feel that if Summer was at a different age at that time, like younger, we wouldn't have been on each others nerves. But luckily Summer and I, learned how to cope and laugh about our new surroundings. We had different habits, but luckily Feng Shui happened. Even though there were still times we wanted to have a door of our own to slam and hide behind. The bathroom door didn't work so well. As soon as she got mad and went in the bathroom and slammed the door behind her, I had to pee of course. I would peck on the door. "Summer! Your mom has to pee."

"Go outside!"

"My pee will turn to an icicle."

"Good! Then you can have something to suck on."

"Summer! Your time is over."

"Mom! It's not fair. When are things going back to normal?"

"After I get to pee. Open the damn door!"

"You peeing isn't gonna get us out of this ridiculous place."

251

"Summer! I'm serious."

"Okay Mom! Whatever!" She opened the door as her eyes slid to the floor. We slid past each other with a slight concern of even brushing upon each other. We were fine the next day as always.

During all these unfortunate situations, including Kathleen's. I was still running the Cafe and it was a real struggle for me. People would say the most stupid things to me. This is definitely where Maw-maw would love to throw out the comment, people don't know the difference between shit and apple butter.

One night I walked over to one table to see how the food was. Then the girl mentioned the fire, when I was getting ready to ask how is your meal. The guy sitting with her looked up and said, "At least the whole thing burnt down." My face and response changed immediately. I was thinking what did you say? What the hell is wrong with you? I didn't say that out loud, because I have a huge filter between my brain and my mouth, unlike some people. I just replied with a smile and tapped the table. "Well, you come back and talk to me when your whole house burns down." and I walked away. He seemed to be a little light on the sauce anyway. Give this boy some apple butter, he wins the stupid prize of the day. How does someone tell you that you should be glad your whole house burnt to the ground.

I was a bitch for about six months and didn't treat people as nicely as I should. I wasn't evil. I was just spitting out some temporary bitterness. One evening I had a waitress to walk in almost crying. She was acting all depressed and whiny when she said. "I lost my camera."

I looked at her with no sympathy on my face. "REALLY!!!! Oh really! That must be awful. Just plain awful! You lost your camera. Boo fucking who!!!"

I hate it that I was that way, but I was. I'm just thankful I snapped out of it and finally returned to my normal bitching at the Cafe. I know this story may get a little deep and trivial and complainy at times. But I will do my best not to stay that way. It's just LIFE.

Life always has a new hand to deal. Sometimes you have to learn to shuffle the deck yourself, so you don't keep playing the same hand over and over. We all have survived some stormy seasons and I feel I've had to cross more than my share of broken bridges. I mean of course, I know everyone has to do some moving around. But, gosh damn it Karma. Get your damn addresses straight.

I guess it has made me try and do things most people would never attempt. Like write these stories. Some people just give a sob story for their lack of giddy up, and that's their reason for failure or lack of motivation. It's just that easy for them to cop out like that. They want to sit back and complain about what wasn't given to them or blame their failures on the ones who raised them, society or what not. Everybody has seen shit, some more than others. No one has actually come from a *Leave it to Beaver* family, except maybe for my dad's, Mom and Dad. I came from a broken home, my parents were young and imperfect and made many parenting mistakes. Its allowed me to grow and become independent, learn different ways of living and not fear a thing. Well almost not a thing, because I just realized I have a phobia. I fear pod flowers! Yes! Pods! Those things are revolting, seriously! I get chills and it makes my stomach roll every time I see one. So florist keep them out of your arrangements. They are frightening. I better not receive any at my funeral, or I will come back and haunt you all, and join Walter and the little girl on one of their escapades. Actually I don't want any flowers, plant a tree please.

But anyway, back to what I was saying. I understand that everyone doesn't get the same advantages and same start. Some people get really, really stuck when they aren't taught any better or have the opportunity to change or get out. Like in that movie 'Gone Baby Gone.' That movie was just plain sad, but true. I'm just saying, if you do know better, and have an opportunity to change things, please don't come crying to me with your pity party.

Would 'I' love to have had a few things different? Yes of course, but they weren't and here I am. I'm glad I got to live in different households, if only to learn that people do things differently and it's okay. It has broaden my views and left me open minded to all situations. As we go through this story, you will notice we all have mishaps. It's all about picking up the pieces. We should look at it like a kid. Build something with Legos. When someone takes them

254

apart or knocks them down, create again. Enjoy the journey, whatever that might be for you.

I'm sure Summer will tell you that I have failed on several occasions and issues as a parent. Like taking care of her when she was sick. She tells people I would stick her in the other room, push her food under the door and spray her with Lysol. That's a little fabricated on her part, but somewhat true. Let me explain. First of all, I handed her the food on a tray, she should have looked at it like room service. Secondly, I sprayed Lysol on the door handles and around the room. She better be glad I didn't stick her in a bubble or put on a hazmat suit. I was just taking precautions. The way I look at it, what was the point in both of us being sick?

My parents have excelled at many good things. They have even come back around full circle and have let me nourish off the tit. You know, that thing you get ripped off of as an infant. Well, I never got to suck on one, period. They were more into trying to burn me, drown me and get me kidnapped. It's all good, it's all good. I started learning at a young age, that sometimes you have to do shit for yourself and for that I thank you Mom and Dad.

Summer on the other hand needs to be pulled off the tit. Everybody needs a tit at one time or another, but you can't suck the sow dry. I want her to have an easier life than myself, but that in itself could maybe back fire. I want her to become self sufficient and have passion for something. I'm trying my best to steer her in the right direction. She needs to learn that shopping and money isn't the key to life. Although money is needed to survive in this world we live in, it isn't everything. She needs to learn that she needs to create her own self fulfilling world and that mommy can't create it for her.

"But Mom! It's expensive out here."

255

"I know this Summer, but if you can't afford to live in this world, create one that you can afford. Act your wage, because I'm not *Wells Fargo*."

Keep in mind this is only her thought as a graduated high school student. Years have passed and she has grown. I don't want her calling me up and screaming, "Mom, why would you say that?" It was just a phase, we all have them.

I just want her to know that peace of mind is learning to live with what we have, and not what we think we should have. Everybody could use a good hand out every now and then. Like when they're down on their luck, but there is a limit. Sometimes you have to bake your own pie and quit asking for a piece of everybody else's.

In saying all that, I don't mean or think you should settle either. You should never settle! Keep reaching for your dreams. But sometimes you just have to except what is and not expect so much and be happy for what you're given. You know, temper your expectations. If you get tired of dragging up an empty bucket out of the well, just move on to another one. Life isn't just black and white, it is an array of colors, just like the rainbow, or a Skittles commercial. Share the rainbow, taste the rainbow and if you don't like what flavor you put in your mouth, spit it out and reach for another.

-Some time's the hardest part, isn't letting go, but rather, learning to start over--Nicole Savahnge ---

Summer and her friend Amanda

Sorry about that major A.D.D. moment, lets get back to the story. One night, Summer had friends over to the garage, while I was working at the Cafe. She came running through the side door, slid around the cooler and came running over to me at the grill. She seemed flustered and there was a huffiness in her voice. "Mom!!!! Who keeps pounding on the garage door?"

"Summer, what are you talking about?"

"Mom someone keeps pounding on the building. Seriously, you guys need to stop, it's freaking us out."

"Summer, it's not anyone over here. We are all way to busy to be worrying about pounding on the garage."

"Well it's really spooky, and whoever is doing it, needs to stop."

We were about to lock horns. "Summer! I'm busy! It's probably one of your friends."

"No!!! Mom! It's not."

"Summer, I have no time for this. Steph! Get your food."

"Why are you ignoring me."

"Summer, I'm not. I'm just trying to get out the food. No one is bothering you."

So she stormed out of the Cafe. I didn't give it another thought, when in fact maybe I should have. A few weeks later when Mom and I were sitting at the bar having our morning coffee, she mentioned that something strange happened to her at the garage. This was before I told her about what Summer said. So I don't think she was making it up. She seemed to be a little freaked out when she said. "Missy, I was in the garage vacuuming and I heard something bang on the wall. I thought maybe it was the beer man or something. So I opened the door and no one was in sight. It was really weird Missy, I felt so uncomfortable."

"That's....so... weird Mom! Summer was just saying the other night, that something was banging on the walls. Wonder what it is?

"Don't know Missy. It really freaked me out over there that day. You think maybe it's Walter, do you think he wants in?"

Knock knock. Who's there? No-body......

It was an icy cold day at the end of January 2009. A wintry mix of weather had settled into central Ky. What began as a light freezing drizzle, turned into sleet and snow. Six inches of snow had accumulated on the ground and the trees were tackled with an inch of ice. Mother Nature had just unleashed an unbelievable amount of winter weather. I swear it was it was cold enough to freeze a fart.

It was Kentucky's hardest hit by an ice storm and the worst natural disaster in our states history. Over 255,000 people were thrown into the dark, and I was one of them. Barack Obama signed a federal declaration for our state. Five thousand utility workers started working around the clock, including the National Guard

I welcome you to Kentucky, the only state, where you wear shorts one day, and a snowsuit the next. Although spring was surely around the corner, old man winter wasn't about to give up without a tussle, and was gonna hand me another challenge to overcome.

The day started like this. After I awoke, I felt the chill on my nose. The fire had once again burned out. When I looked out the garage door, I noticed the ice thickening and clinging to everything. When I went to open the doors they were frozen harder than a brick bat. I tugged and jerked till I finally broke the bond. I stepped out the door to get a closer look. Yep! We had been hit. Hit hard.

I stepped back in to turn on the TV to check the news, that's when I noticed that my power was out. The first thing that ran through my head was, oh shit! The Cafe, the meat, it's gonna ruin. I had to make a plan, and a quick one at that. Me, being in the middle of nowhere, I knew I had better take care of my own business. Summer and I were gonna become prisoners here if I didn't act fast, even though authorities were recommending everyone stay put.

I didn't want Summer to be stuck in the garage all day without power, while I was running around searching for a generator to hook up at the Cafe. Plus, how was she gonna stay warm? She wouldn't have had the first clue on how to keep the fire going. So I woke her and asked her to call a friend, and see if they had power. "Why, Mommy? What's wrong? What's going on? How bad is it? What are we gonna do?" Keep in mind Summer talks so fast sometimes I can't even understand what she just said. She has a gift to gab, rat-a-tat-tat. She can deliver information at the speed of light sometimes, and talks fully caffeinated. I'm constantly having to say, slow down tiger, just so I can grasp what she is saying. As she was calling around friend to friend, she was still speaking in her silver tongue.

Just a tad bit of information: Psychologist say, talking fast can be a magic bullet when trying to convince someone into something, because they don't have the time to process or argue. No wonder her friends does what she wants.

So after she got ready, we headed out the door. We slid across the slickery ice and hopped in the truck. I locked it in four wheel drive, took a deep breath and said. "Look out icy roads, here we come." Summer was a nervous wreck. "Mommy, please be safe."

I drove her over to her friends and dropped her off at the mailbox. Just kidding, I gave her front door service, kissed her and said I love you, see ya soon. Kristen called while I was on my way to town and said that they were setting up camp in her mom and dads generated powered barn and that Summer and I should come over. I told her that I had already dropped Summer off, but I would be over as soon as I got my task done.

Although the terrain was tough, the beauty of it all was astonishing. I mean breath taking. The trees were engulfed in crystal, and was shining bright as the brightest thing you or I could imagine.

261

Like I really can not describe it. It was the most beautiful and disastrous sight, all at the same time.

The brute power of Mother Nature had shown its face, but I had a task to do, even though the elements around me were against me. I chose to make it an adventure and explore the beauty. Summer was safe, so I was good to go.

There were still a few people in town with power, very few. My friend happened to be one of them. I headed straight there for the generator, dodging falling trees along the way. I was standing there in the icy cold shaking like a leaf, waiting for him to load it. It started to sound like the brawny man was on a rampage and clearing the whole town of trees. There was sure to be no shortage of paper towels soon.

I was trembling when I asked. "How in the hell do you guys still have power?"

"We probably won't have it for long at this rate." Right at that very moment, a thirty foot tree came tumbling down, missing my truck by inches.

"Holy crap dude, I got to get out of here."

"Missy, this thing hasn't been started in a while, lets make sure it works." He tugged and pulled and it wouldn't start of course. "This damn thing isn't gonna start."

"Hey, I will call Kevin, my neighbor. He is good at these things."

So I reached in my winter jacket for my cell phone and gave him a call. Luckily he was home and said he would give it his best. We loaded it up in the back of my SUV and off I went. It had slipped my mind that Kevin lived at the top of a very, I mean very, steep hill, with a lake right in the curve of his driveway. What was I thinking? My cousin Kristen had already sacrificed one car to the lake. (Kevin just happens to be the father of Kristen's daughter Kaitlin, ain't nothing like adding another little turd to the pile of the family. Obviously they were doing the hanky panky when I was frog gigging with them. Guess they wanted their own bundle of joy.)

So when I got to the end of the drive, I was nervous as hell. I stared down the challenge. I thought to myself. Self! You can do this. I double checked my 4-wheel drive and headed up the curvy crooked driveway, while holding my butt cheeks tight. What good that did, I have no idea, just came with the challenge, my ass was so tight, I bet you couldn't have even got a pen in there. I was determined to make it to the top, and that I did. But not without creating a muscle spasm in my ass.

When I pulled up he was standing at the garage doors and helped me unload. As he was working on it, I began to get more and more nervous. The trees were cracking all around us. Sounded like Bigfoot was wrestling someone in the woods. My patience were wearing thin.

"Hurry! I'm never gonna get outta' here Kevin!"

"Oh you'll be alright!" as he laughed. Trust me Kevin is not one to get excited about anything.

"No, seriously Kevin. I got to get this to the Cafe and get everything hooked up and get over to Kristen's barn where they are setting up ice camp. I can't get stuck here or at my place."

He was kneeling at the generator. "Why don't you just set all your meat outside? It's cold enough." I looked down at him and simply stated in a sarcastic, elongated, monotone voice. "NO!" The same way my dad would say it, when I asked him to do something that he wasn't willing to do. It's no, times ten. Just no.

Kevin just looked at me and smiled. "I was only joking, I know the coyotes would eat it all."

"Not just that Kevin, it's food safety too, you fool."

"Yeah! Yeah! Why you being so serious right now?"

"Maybe because a natural disaster is happening around us, and I got shit to take care of, and my butt muscle still hurts from coming up your drive."

"Damn, this thing hasn't been started forever, has it?" He continued to tug and pull. "You sure you don't want to set your food outside?" as he looked at me and laughed. But with one last pull, it started and black smoke swarmed his face.

"Yay! Awesome, it started. Thanks! But one last request Kevin."

"And what might that be?"

"You have to follow me. I'm scared of your hill and I will never get that thing started back without you."

"Okay, Missy, I will follow you, you big scaredy cat. Does this mean I get free steaks for a month?"

So, many hours after I started my quest, it was starting to pay off. The day had already turned into nightfall. What seems like a short quick story to you, was actually a day long journey for me. We finally got to the Cafe and got everything hooked up.

"Missy you gonna be okay?" He asked with concern.

"Yep! I just got to grab some clothes and head over to ice camp."

It was so dark outside, I mean pitch black. I watched Kevin's tail lights leave the driveway. I ran into the garage to grab some clothes, using my cell phone to find my way. The trees were still breaking all around me. My heart started to race, I think I was so scared I may have only grabbed a toothbrush. I ran back out and hopped in my truck and took off down my one lane road. Not but about a half mile up the road, I had to hit the brakes, as I slid off the road. There was what looked to be a hundred year old tree, sprawled completely across the road, fence line to fence line. I hit the steering wheel and said. Are you f****** kidding me? Is this real life? A big fat ass tree. What the hell? This just had to happen! I was right on Kevin's heels. How the hell did this happen so fast? Yes, I was talking to myself, but I was not answering. As I was backing up, I called my cuz Kristen.

Have I told who Kristen is yet? I mean I did introduce her in the first story. She is the one who went frog gigging with me. She is older now and reminds me of 'Chelsea Handler' and 'Jamie Lee Presley. She has Chelsea's sarcasm and that redneck twang of Jamie. She has the looks of them combined. She would be the epitome of both of them, if they were to have a baby.

Speaking of baby: Here goes a by the way, that reminds me moment.

Mom told me that when Kristen was born, she didn't have any eyebrows. Mom said, when she looked at her, she said she couldn't tell which end was which. The doctor didn't even know which end to spank, her face or her butt. Then Mom, preceded to say. I don't know what happened to that baby! She was so ugly! Thought we was gonna have a little alien on our hands. Not today of course, but we sure were worried as hell back then.

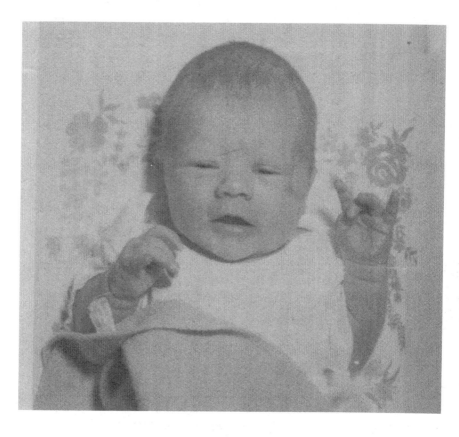

POOR KRISTEN!!

Thank goodness they grew.

Anyway, back to the story. I was telling Kristen, I wasn't gonna to make it over.

"Why not?" she said.

"Because there is a huge ass tree, right in the middle of the road, and I can't get through."

"Awww... Really!!! as she sounded disappointed. "You can't get past at all."

"Nope! Sure can't."

"Don't you have 4-wheel drive? Put'er down in gear and get on over here."

"I can't get through fence lines and over a huge ass tree."

"So what cha gonna do, Hoochie?"

"Well hooker, I'm just gonna head back to the garage. I think I will start a fire, light a candle, have a glass of wine and sleep naked. Especially since I haven't had any privacy since Summer and I got shoved into the garage together. I'm gonna take advantage of my privacy."

"Sounds like your planning a romantic evening with yourself. You gonna take advantage of your privacy or your private parts?"

"Shut up Kristen."

I could hear her laughing, which was unusual, she usually doesn't make any sound when she laughs. "Well, call me if you need anything, even though I can't get to you, I will sling shot it through the field."

"Yeah, yeah, whatever! I will holler at you tomorrow."

So I drove back and did just what I said I was gonna do. Not what she assumed I was gonna do. I was an ice prisoner, actually to my much delight. So I thought!

I could still hear all the ruckus in the knobs around me. Geeez!!!! Is there gonna be any forest left in the morning, I thought to myself. I had to think to myself, because there was no one there to say it to, except maybe for Walter.

But, I was soon fast asleep from the warmth of the fire. I believe I was dreaming that old man winter was having a little fun with mother nature and creating me some spring. BAM! BAM! BAM!

BAM! I was abruptly woken by a knock on the door. I jumped from my bed. 'Who the fuck?' I knew it wasn't anyone telling me my house was on fire, for I didn't have one. I knew it wasn't anyone I knew, cause they couldn't get through. My gut just knew not to answer the door. There was still a candle burning from earlier. I franticly wrapped the blanket around me, grabbed my phone and darted to the bathroom, like a groundhog running back in its hole. I shut the door and looked at my phone, it was three in the morning. Holy shit! What is it? What's going on? Who is knocking at my door? If it was someone I knew, they would be calling my name. What the hell? How would they have got down this road anyway? I was scrambling and in a complete panic and fearing for my safety.

I called Kristen immediately. I could barely hold the phone in my hand from trembling. "Hello?" She answered with a sleeping frog in her throat.

"OMG, Kristen! I'm freaking out! I'm so scared, you got to come get me."

"What is it? Why in the Sam carnation are you calling me this late? I hope it's important."

"Someone or something just banged at my door. Sounded like they were trying to knock it down to get in or something."

"You sure it's not the ice falling Missy?"

My voice started to raise and my hands were still trembling.

"I don't fucking think so Kristen. Ice don't go Bam! Bam! Bam! I have never been this scared before. You know me, I'm not scared of anything."

"Just calm down Missy."

"That's easy for you to say."

"Look out your door."

269

"I don't wanna. I don't know who or what is out there. Plus, I can't run or even get out of my road if I wanted to. I'm naked and that huge ass tree has me trapped in."

"Missy, you gotta check."

"Fine, whatever!"

I ducked out the bathroom door and into the kitchen part of our little living space. I tried to scramble and sneak to find a flashlight. I was rummaging through the drawer. Yes, we only had one.

"Kristen! I'm naked! I'm scared!"

"Well, run outside, that should scare them off."

"Shut up! Listen! All I can find, is a little fucking 3inch energizer bunny, kiddy, fucking flashlight. Oh shit! My phone is going dead. You gotta' figure a way to get over here, and now! You know I have a shady character that lives at the end of my road. My dead end road may I remind you."

"Maybe its Keyda," as she laughed.

"Really Kristen! My dog banging on my door, I don't think so! Why is everyone trying to be a comedian today? You and Steve need to break out the chainsaws and come and get me."

"Missy, you sure you're not hallucinating from all the shit that's been going on? You sure it wasn't in your sleep, before I wake up Steve."

"Kristen, I'm gonna kill you if you don't get here yesterday."

"OK! I will try to wake Steve up."

"Hurry! I'm not playing, this is messed up! Something is up! It's not the ice... or Keyda.... You know about the Walter situation, and that mother fucker wants in here NOW! Hurry up, please

When we hung up I knew she wasn't taking me seriously. I slid on some clothes, not knowing if someone was watching me or not. There was only one window, but it was enough to look into this little place. I was holding my phone in one hand and my big flashlight in the other, ha-ha NOT! About ten minutes later, my phone rings. "We can't get through!"

"What!!" I screamed. "Have you tried the chainsaw?"

"The tree is too big. We would be here all night. Look out your door and see if you can see our headlights. We are right over the hill."

"Kristen, I don't want to look out."

"Missy you have to."

"I tell you what! If someone is out there, you and Steve better come plowing through the fields and get me. If you don't see my headlights come on in five seconds, your ass better be here! I mean it Kristen!"

So I slowly opened the blinds and peeked through. I could see their headlights through the mist up the road. No sign of Keyda, no trace of falling ice. I opened the door to take a better look, but no foot prints either. I shut my door back and hit remote start on my truck. "OK I see you! I'm gonna make a run for my truck, but I'm telling you again. If I'm not there in ten seconds, you better be ready to turn into Hercules, Popeye, whoever the hell you wanna be and save my ass."

Fast as lightning, I made a mad dash toward my truck. My feet were trying to come out from under me as I slipped around on the ice. Luckily my truck didn't have much ice on it, because I had been in it earlier and it hadn't completely frozen back over yet. I spun out of the driveway, and went speeding up the road, as fast as you can drive on ice, sliding side to side. I about slammed into the fallin tree, but stopped just short of it. I backed up and pulled my truck over to the side of the road in my neighbor's yard. I jumped out and hurdled through the tree like an agile monkey. I jumped in the back seat of

Steve's truck. Kaitlin, which is Kristen's daughter was in the back seat and looked over with big wide open eyes. "Oh My Gosh Missy! What's going on? You're scaring me."

"Shewl, I don't know, lets just get outta' here."

Kristen laughs in her almost silent giggle. Then I smack her on the back of the head. "Haha! Back at you Kristen. Sure it's funny. I just had the scare of my life and for some reason you think it's funny. Maybe you think I've had scarier things to happen to me before. But this shit is different. I just got a bad vibe about this, a skin chilling vibe. I don't think I've ever been that scared. I was stuck by myself, literally stuck."

"Well, I'm sure it's scary, but you're with us now."

"Yeah, I guess with the house burning and Conrad telling me about Walter didn't help much either. Also Summer and Mom have had experiences with something or nothing beating on the door."

"Nothing! How does nothing beat on the door?"

"Nothing! Whatever! It's fine! Its all good! Let's head on over to ice camp."

About that time, the milk farmer came sliding down the road in his big truck. He jumped out observing the situation. I rolled down my window. "What are you doing here?"

"Got cows to milk, and it can't wait. Their tits will explode from here to Kalamazoo," the farmer said.

"Oh! That wouldn't be good. How you gonna get back there? How you gonna get through that tree? We couldn't get through."

"Watch me!" the farmer said.

"Can I help?" Steve offered. "I got a chainsaw in the back."

So they fired up the chainsaw and began cutting. Just a few minutes into cutting, he had only removed a small portion. Steve set down the chainsaw. "This is gonna take forever."

The farmer got impatient and he got in his truck and basically plowed right through it. He was as determined as me to get through that tree, obviously even more so. Guess he didn't want his cows tits to explode. That would be a sight. Now wouldn't it?

"You wanna go through there and get your truck?" Steve asked.

"Uh NO! Did you just see what he did to his truck? I will just get it later. Come on, lets just go."

"Ice camp it is." Kristen replied.

We all were gonna have a mutual excuse for days to do absolutely nothing. The storm had interrupted my business, but it was a good excuse to play in the snow or ice. While shaken up from this middle of the night wonder and terror, we were all still a little giddy.

So when we arrive at Ice Camp, which is Kristen's parent's, Kathleen and Danny's barn/garage. It sets behind their historic cabin. As we walked around the cabin to enter ice camp, there was a sign of activity coming from inside the cabin. It wasn't Kathleen because she was still in the hospital. It seemed to be a ghostly shadow moving across the top of the second floor bedroom window. The ROOM where Kathleen herself had told the story about something grabbing her son, Little Danny, during his sleep. Kaitlin and I both screamed and ran into the barn.

"Oh my God Missy, I'm so scared!" Kaitlin screamed.

"WTF!!! What was it?" I yelled.

"I don't know Missy," Kaitlin replied with her hands over her mouth. Kristen was giggling with more silent laughter.

"Why are you laughing, Mom?" Kaitlin asked.

"I don't know, but that shit is funny. You should have seen you girls about knock each other down to get in."

"You guys better not be messing with me. This whole day has been crazy." I said.

I don't know why she was laughing again. Maybe she has nervous laughter like Summer, because she had to be as scared as we were. Kristen had previously told me about some spooky stories on the old cabin. The cabin is at least 200 years old, and it has been told that spirits are in there. Not that I'm a true believer, but I definitely don't disbelieve either, especially after all the shit that has happened in and to my house. I think my mind just changed in a tip of a hat or may I say, at the bang of a door.

Just a few short minute later, we were a curled up on the couches with blankets over our heads. Like that was really gonna help. Kristen peeks out and started telling Kaitlin and I about a phone call she had received at her mom's house one day. Guess she felt she needed to scare us a little bit more. "Oh... Missy, it was so weird and scary. I don't really know how to describe it. There were all kinds of voices on the phone. High pitched with some static and low voices talking over top each other at the same time, and it scared me so bad. I mean, I was like fully awake. I told Mom and Dad, and they were like, oh you were dreaming, and I was like, no! It really was something. Well, two weeks later. Well, in between then, let me tell you this first. We had a dog. The dog started growling at its dog food."

I laughed and said. "Was you feeding it Purina?"

"No, Missy, shut up. They ended up having to kill that dog, because it went off."

"Where did it go to?" I asked.

"Missy, damn it. Let me finish my story. It use to help Dad get the cows up. They were trying to get them up one day and it was just crazy. Kevin was over here helping em, and that dog got loose and started attacking like four hundred and five hundred pound calves. I mean gettin' um down by their throats.... So finally they caught it, and it bit Kevin on his arm and ripping it. They ended up shooting that dog that day. Ummm... I forgot to tell you this part, just a few days after I got the call, Mom had the same phone call. She was home by herself. She was awake. Gives me goose bumps just thinking about it right now." She started to rub her arms." It was like eight in the morning. She said you can't describe what it sounds like, but she did hear them. They said something about the dog, and that dog started going off. I guess it was two weeks after that we had to shoot it."

As I listened intensely to that long winded story, I jump up from the blankets. "Well Kristen, that's like the cat I got right before the house burnt down. I cant stand it, I call it psycho cat. I haven't liked it since day one, it freaking barked at me one day.

Kristen and Kaitlin busted out in laughter. "Hahahahah, it barked at you? Yeah right."

"No! Seriously, it was weird, ask Nicole. It ran up behind her one day and bit her ankle. She will tell you, I swear. I swear that cat has a spirit in it, and I do mean that. Reminds me of that movie *"Fallen"* that *Denzel Washington* is in. You know, when the cat walked away in the end, with the devil in it as they were playing that weird song, *Sympathy for the Devil Lyrics."* I started to sing. "Pleased to meet you, hope you guess my name….. Oh yeah. Ah! What's puzzling you? Is the nature of my game, oh yeah (woo, woo! woo woo!)"

Kristen laughs. "I definitely think some animals have some kind of sixth sense and make sure you don't quit your day job.."

"I do too and I won't."

"Missy, you know Toby down here at my moms. I swear, he is evil." (Toby is a ittsy bitsy dog, with little dog syndrome and a Pitt-bull attitude.)

I look Kristen straight in the face. "That dog is evil. I hate that dog with a passion. It bit my dad's ankle and I can't go in the garage unless I have a fire poker in my hand to keep it away. It's the meanest looking little dog I've ever seen. Where is that little fucker anyway?"

Kristen replies, "It's in the house."

"Well, that movement could have been the dog"

"Missy, he isn't tall enough, he barely reaches the bottom of the curtain. My mom never even touches that dog. It follows my mom everywhere. What kind of animal bonds with somebody like that? She never does anything for it. She doesn't feed it... or pet.... it or anything."

Kaitlin peeks her head out. "Maybe hits it."

We all start laughing.

 "Yeah, she will be mean to it. She hit's it with a fly swatter. I swear Missy, it's crazy."

As I'm still laughing, "maybe they're both the devil."

Kaitlin Jumps out from the covers. "Missy you better not let my Maw-maw hear you say that." As she covers her mouth with her hands. "Oh my mom! Maw-maw is a witch and Toby is her Witch Lore. He is helping her practice magic."

Kristen stares at her like she is stupid. "Whatever Kaitlin, I don't think so. But Missy, she throws fruit at it, oranges and everything, seriously!!! I think it knew that, like, she was gonna have an aneurysm or something. I swear I do. Like those dogs that can signal when someone has epilepsy. That's why it stays by her."

276

"Yeah, maybe kinda like on TV the other day. They had this cat in a nursing home and it went to someone's bed. They would die in the next few days. They said the cat could sense death

Kristin shockingly said. "Oh My Gosh... I wouldn't want it coming to my bed," then started laughing.

"Hell no, me either. But seriously, they will go lay with them. Animals have a sense like that. Animals know when to leave when a hurricane or something is coming, even birds seek shelter before the storm. They just know that shit, wish I did. Sometimes you just have to be surprised, shit your pants, wipe your ass and move on."

I THINK I'LL JUST BE HAPPY TODAY.

"It may be unfair, but what happens in a few days, sometimes even a single day, can change the course of a whole lifetime."
Khaled Hosseini

The up coming picture, is of me standing in front of my house, or let's say lack of house. I'm wearing a set of clothes that someone brought to me. I'm also wearing my Met's hat, that I found in the garage, from back when I played little league.

"When we least expect it, life sets us a challenge to test our courage and willingness to change; at such a moment, there is no point in pretending that nothing has happened or in saying that we are not yet ready. The challenge will not wait. Life does not look back. A week is more than enough time for us to decide whether or not to accept our destiny." Paulo Coelho

So as we move on, this story will now bring us to spring of 2009. Everyone has a worse nightmare, and one of mine had just recently happened. No, Not the scary night, but the fact I had just lost my home. But still a challenge was in order. I had to get my shit together and it was time for me to get a skip back into my step. So thanks to the shoe, I decided to go forward and draw the plans for my new house, while on Xanax, mind you. I had a plan in mind and I had to get out of the garage before Summer and I started playing Wack-a-moe on each others heads.

When I finally completed the plans, I had to take them to an architect to get it drawn for the builders. I, myself, didn't know how to draw the pitch, you know, the angle for the roof. So I needed professional help, for the first time. Just kidding, I've had professional help before. If things keep up like this, I might need what some people would call for real professional help.

One day on my way home, the builders were working on the house. As I popped up over the hill, I looked down toward my land. I could see something that looked to resemble a church steeple. HALLELUJAH, HALLELUJAH...Holy shit....it was the top of my house. They were putting the rafters up. I pulled in the drive and got out and walked up to one of the carpenters.

"What on God's green earth is going on here? Why is that so high? It looks like a church! Why is it so high and pointy? Who needs a roof that tall?"

"Well, that's what's on your drawing, a New England style roof. You planning on getting a lot of snow?" the man said.

"You never know. We did just have that crazy ass ice storm of a lifetime, but no. That wasn't my plan. It didn't look that tall in the plans. That's crazy

"Well, you want us to take it down?" As he replied with a hint of smart ass.

"How much is it gonna cost to do that?"

"I would say, a right pretty penny. We can stop and give you a day to think about it."

"Okay! Let's do that!" So I slept on it. The next day I decided to go ahead with the amazingly large church roof. At least if we have another ice storm like the previous one, I won't have to worry about my roof caving in.

Everyone that came into the Cafe would ask me. Are you building a church over there? It was aggravating the shit out of me. It looked even higher after they put the plywood on. I decided to climb up into the top of it. You could only get there by a ladder. I stood up and looked at the guy. "Jesus Christ, this could be a whole nother house and this is just the attic."

"Yes ma'am it is." The builder replied.

"Well, we're gonna have to do something with this space. We need to be resourceful, this is insane. What wasted space."

So that night, I brainstormed. I drew up a plan to make another loft, coming out of the bedroom upstairs. I thought it would be a great idea to make it into a Rock Band Room for Summer. Maybe this room was a blessing in disguise. I never had a problem with noise in our other house. It was like a modernized ranch house, it was large and spaced out. I never even knew when she had company. Well, I knew, I just didn't have to hear them.

I had only drawn out 1800 feet of space, for the new house, which should be plenty for two girls like ourselves. The plan was as you walk in, to the left was going to be a spiral staircase going to the upstairs. The kitchen was going to be open and connect to the living room. There is no ceiling in the kitchen, I left it out because I still wanted my loft feel. Large windows completely surround the house, so I could view my surroundings. There was is bed and bath downstairs along with a laundry room. Upstairs an open computer room looking over the kitchen. Summers bed and bath was to be up there too. Of course another loft, with a very, very small spiral staircase, that leads to the church steeple.

I told her once. I hope all your friends are skinny, because they're not getting up they're if their not. Her mouth just about hit the floor right before she said, "Mom...."

"Oh whatever Summer, it's true. Girl you know its true, ooohh oohh ohhh I love you."

"Mom, don't quit your day job."

'Damn! I must sing as bad as *Milli Vanilli*' Oh! That's right they don't sing, imposters.

I decided to put a Jacuzzi tub in Summers bathroom. Bad idea, I mean bad idea. Bad ideas were plaguing me. I had one in the other house, but it was downstairs. Never gave thought to the problem it would cause being upstairs. I was watching TV one night and she decided to use it for the first time. When she turned it on, I thought the house was going to fall apart. I had no idea what the noise was at first, but it was something awful sounding. The walls were vibrating and it sounded like a dope chopper had invaded my house.

Speaking of dope choppers, we have aerial raids every year when harvesting time comes around. People around here scatter like mice when you walk into a barn, when those suckers start flying over. Soon we will talk more about this invasion, that happens out here in Timbuctoo.

But for now, back to when they were building our house. Summer and I walked in one day, just to see how far they had gotten. The house was empty, with bare walls. When we walked in, we heard a weird noise. It was a knocking sound. We stopped dead in our tracks, took each others hand and just stared at each other. Not a movement from either of us, motionless like a praying mantis waiting to ambush.

Then just a few seconds later, Summer looked at me with startled eyes. "Mom... What is it?"

I was quite startled myself. "I'm not sure."

"Is it our ghost?"

"I don't think he would have moved back in that fast, but I guess he didn't have to pack." I said with a giggle.

"Mom... Seriously, it's not funny."

"Summer I'm sure there is an explanation for it, but it is quite spooky sounding, isn't it?"

"I'm going back to the garage." Off she went. Elvis had left the building.

I started to investigate because all homes have a history, but this house was new. What the hell could it be? Had something else already taken up residency? Was there an explanation for the noise? This time.....There was. The wind was blowing hard that day. The air vent they had put in the bathroom ran outside. It had a flap on it, and the wind was making it come open and then fly shut. There isn't too many things around here that can be explained away that easy. It's about a fifty-fifty situation. It's funny that we were frightened for that moment. So much spooky unexplained shit has happened, that just the simple stuff can spook us sometimes. Then we blow it off and continue our day, not much we can do about it.

*After reading my rough draft. Beverly came to the conclusion
that it was my deceased spelling teacher haunting me. Trying to
make amends, for falsifying my spelling records. She asked me if
there was a statute of limitations on suing the school, for letting me
graduate without learning to spell. Beverly, Beverly, Beverly, you're
cracking me up. Yes, I know my spelling is bad, that's what I have
you for.*

As spring ripened into summer, everyone was out enjoying the
beautiful weather. I've always needed projects to keep my head
busy. That's just the way I'm built. But this one I was not looking
forward to. My whole summer was spent in Lowe's. I was ready to
blow my brains out, it was a miserable. I had to pick everything out
from what color light switches, to the color of paint and everything
in between. I was so mad and depressed at the same time. My
feeling's were so displaced and all over the place. You just feel
naked and stripped of yourself. I had just done all of this. My other
house was just the way I wanted it, and I had done it all myself,
except for the main structure. Everything from laying tile, wood
floors, dry walling, building a fireplace and on and on. There were so
many memories in that home. People would tell me, but you get to
buy new stuff. I didn't need new stuff, you fool.

Moving along. I had lots and lots of huge windows and so does
my house today. It's a house of glass. People says it looks like it
should be sitting on a beach somewhere instead of in the middle of a
hay pasture full of cows. I use to have the coolest picture ever. It was
of some friends laying out by the pool sunbathing, while sixty cows
stared at them across the fence line.

In the kitchen of the old house, I decided to remodel the ceiling
like a wood floor. While in the process of staining the wood,

284

Summer walked across it and left her little precious footprints on most of the boards. Did I get upset? For a moment. Then I thought what the hell, I will put them up anyway, foot prints and all. When friends or family would look up and see it, I could see the thoughts on their face. I would just laugh and tell them the story.

My home wasn't done perfect, but it was done by me, and each and every mistake had a story. That's why I loved our home so much. But I'm getting really good at learning, that the past should be left in the past. Otherwise it can, and will destroy my future. I'm trying to live life for what today and maybe tomorrow has to hold, not for what yesterday has taken away. If you think about it real hard, yesterday and tomorrow really don't exist anyway, only if you think about it real hard, I mean real hard. You don't have to think about it, if you don't want. I'm not here to strain your brain. So lets just be happy today.

You must admit, you can only feel what you are feeling at the moment. THAT'S IT. You can talk about what you felt, but you don't feel it anymore. You can think about what's gonna happen tomorrow, but yet, you don't feel that either. You're just assuming. You think about it, but it never feels the same as you thought it might. I mean, it might once in a blue moon, but I wouldn't bank on it. So let it all go and enjoy the moment. It's all we have and all we are guaranteed.

I got the new house built in the amount of time it takes to have a baby, and yes that would be your usual nine months. Even though I was stunned, I still had the perseverance to move on and getter done. Guess I find comfort being in overdrive, even though there were times I wanted to crawl in a hole. I can handle it, until I can't.

Joe Mack, thinks, I'm like a cow out in the field. One who would run into the electric fence, over and over again no matter how much it hurts, just trying to escape or get to the molasses bucket. He says I just can't stand to be contained. He is right, I don't like to be contained. Some people consider it a good thing. Then there is my Aunt Beverly who thinks it's just a dumb cow. She could be right about that particular cow, but I look at it like the cow is going for what it wants, no matter the cost. We all have points of views.

Through it all, I was still wondering how I had arrived at this place in my life. My life has been like my house. I had a vision and designed it a certain way, but the builders built something a little different, but it was still beautiful. Just like my life, not what I picture. Just glad that chapter is over. Always know that your struggles develop your strengths, if you make the choice not to surrender and just be happy today.

"Once you put the pieces back together, even though you may look intact, you were never quite the same as you'd been before the fall." --Jodi Picoult.--

"The truth is, unless you let go, unless you forgive yourself, unless you forgive the situation, unless you realize the situation is over, you cannot move forward." --Steve Marbaboli--

New House

Summer and I finally moved over to the new house. Yay! We were out of the garage without any bumps or bruises. Neither one of us murdered the other. We were gonna have our own bedrooms once again, with doors to slam. I had bought a bed for me, a bed for her, a kitchen table, a couch and a television. That was it, that's all we needed I thought. Until the first night I stayed there. I awoke to Mom and Beverly pecking on my window. Hands and faces stuck to the window peeking and laughing at me while I slept. At least they didn't have lip stick smeared all over their faces, like Grandma. Although it wouldn't have surprised me if she did. Mom has been known to do some crazy shit too. I remember she walked into the Cafe one day right before it opened. She had put her dress on backwards, smudged her lipstick and teased her hair high up on her

287

head. She came strutting in and asked everyone if they thought she looked good for her date. Someone replied that she looked like a raped whore.

But back to the window. They were just staring at me. I jumped up out of bed, threw on some clothes and out the door I went.

"Where are you going?" they yelled.

"To Lowe's again, to get curtains. My first set of curtains. Didn't need them in the other house, but obviously I do in this one." I really didn't have curtains in the other house. The way it set, we just didn't need them. Plus, why pay to have curtains, when you have beautiful windows and want to see outside and experience natures wonders.

One night, I was lying on the couch, just chillin' and watching television, when all of a sudden I heard a noise that sounded like a ghost done crawled up inside a dying cow. Mmmmrrrrrrr, Mmmmrrrrrrrrrr. It was quite unnerving for some reason. I got up and walked around slowly investigating. I looked out the window, because my first thought was maybe dad had a cow dying, or maybe he took the calves away from their mommas. They cry for days when he does that. It is quite creepy out here in the middle of nowhere land, listening to them down in the holler. None of that was the case. So I was confused as I walked on over toward the kitchen area as the noise persisted. I slowly put my ear toward my new fridge, the noise was coming from inside. Why in the hell does it sound like a dying cow or some kind of monster out of a Stephen King novel. No answers were found, it just made the noise till it didn't.

Summer started fading into fall and the witching month was upon us. Summer and I had only been in the house for a couple months. I woke up one morning and went to turn on the light, didn't work. Got a bulb, didn't work. Went to turn on the TV, didn't work.

So I called Mom at the Cafe and asked her if she had power over there, and indeed she did. Then I called Kathleen and she did too. She asked if I was hit by lightning or something. I wasn't sure, I wasn't awakened through the night. You think I would have heard something, but I didn't and the situation was curious. Everything was toast and I still don't know why. Thing's were really getting strange. Maybe it was time to call the ghost busters.

Just know that insurance companies hate me. It wasn't the first claim nor the second. I've had five, that's just the house, vehicles excluded. I'm hungry, be back soon to try and tie up this story.

MAY BEE CONTINUED.

Okay Readers, here comes the long awaited story! Maybe you already forgot the ending to the first book. You forgot about the insinuated ghost, didn't you? Now you can believe this or not. I'm not asking you to believe anything. I myself, believe in everything, to a certain extent. I think anything is possible. But this is how things started and continued to happen, and if you think I'm exaggerating, I'm not.

This may be the answer I've been looking for! Or was it? Maybe I don't need to know this. Do I wanna know this? Do you wanna know this? Are you even gonna believe this? I haven't lied to you yet, I promise. I'm sure we will get into stories overlapping stories, but I'm gonna write it as I research, remember, and think of it. This story may be going in a completely different direction than I thought. Things are getting very interesting and bone chilling at the same time, as I continue to make shocking discoveries.

Everything seemed normal around the new house for a while. Things had seemed to calm down a bit since the second Halloween party and the burning of my house. May I remind you I said a bit, not totally. I didn't buy any clocks to hang, because I knew they wouldn't work anyway. Let me tell you this real quick. For Christmas a few years back I gave Joe Eddie a cool Rolling Rock clock that hung in the Cafe. I had taken it to the house to wrap it, maybe that was a mistake. Why? Because mom called me immediately once they got home. "Joe Eddie said you can have this clock back."

"Why?"

"The hands are rolling backwards."

"That's weird. I've never seen one go backwards."

"We don't want this crazy thing over here. You can have your ghost back."

"Mom! Maybe Joe Eddie hung it up backwards or something."

"Joe Eddie would never do that goony!"

That for sure was an unexplained phenomenon. Just like the crazy cat, oh yes, you know the one. I think he disappeared to the barn after the fire. But he's back... He sits up on the edge of the deck staring into the window, like he is looking at something over my shoulder. It's very eery. When it makes its appearance at the Cafe, it's usually from the top of the roof. How he gets up there I have no idea. When we walk out after work, there he is staring and shrieking out his meow, as the wind blows through its thick brown and black tangled up hair. It looks like a bad Donald Trump comb over. He truly looks possessed. So does the cat.

Back in the other house every now and then I would smell a slight hint of sewage or rotting flesh. It was so stinky and so

290

peculiar, because the smell would just come and go. But every time I called the plumber to check out the situation, he couldn't find anything wrong. What that has to do with what? I don't know. It just reminded me of some of the haunted movies I've watched over the years. They say ghost usually had a peculiar smell. Believe if you would, but I have been frightened and fascinated simultaneously. It makes my bones shiver, and my friends too. Which brings us back to the past few years. I've been doing some research, in my spare time on why, my house burnt completely to the ground. I want to know what was the common denominator. Not even the fire inspectors could tell me. They just threw up their hands and said, I don't know, just collect your money and move on.

I've talked to mom about it several times. I just find it curious that she and I have been around so many fires. Once again over morning coffee, I look at her suspiciously. "Haven't you been around during all these fires? Anybody question you yet?"

"Don't be looking at me young lady! Maybe you started lighting fires like the little girl in that movie, Fire Starter."

"Whatever Mom!"

"Well, You've been around during all of them too. Can't help it if you were just a baby the first time." As we both started to laugh.

So, I was gonna find out why all this weird shit happens around here. I never knew exactly who Walter was, I only knew that he had died in the house. So I decided to walk over to my neighbors one day to get more information on the situation. Miss Conrad was sitting outside by the garage in a lawn chair. I started the conversation with a ghost story. Haunting of some sort. Before I realized, she said Walter was her dad. I started to change my words and what my interest were immediately. I was retracting my story and reeling it in

291

like you would a fishing line. I didn't want her to think I thought her dad was a ghost. I just stood there swaying back and fourth. I thought I had gotten the job done and went on to ask. "So, may I ask what happen to your dad? Conrad had told me he died in my house."

"Well, honey, he went back to the barn one day. When he came home he was feeling really bad, and he died later that night of a heart attack in the front bedroom."

"Oh! That is terrible! I'm sorry to hear that."

"But, honey, I don't think there were ever any ghost over there though."

Oh shit!!! I thought to myself. She did get what I was implying. Obviously! I had said just enough to her, that she knew I was speaking of a ghost. I was calling her dad a ghost. Not cool.

Then she said. "But....there was this one weird thing that used to happen over there. Blue glass use to always come up in our back yard, every time it would rain. We moved over there when they built that house, after the previous one that stood there burnt down."

"Oh shit! Wow! Another house burnt there? When?"

She slightly shook her head. "I'm not sure, it was back when I was young. You could maybe ask Conrad, he might know, but he isn't home at the moment

"Well..... Miss Conrad, I got to head to work. Thanks for talking with me, hope you enjoying the rest of your day."

I never went back over to talk to them about it. It always takes time to investigate and I just can't find the time. Especially with the Cafe, the writing, Summer, and a girlfriend, then not a girlfriend. LIFE. Remember it gets in the way. Like today, I hit a deer. (Them damn deer are definitely suicidal around here.) Insurance called. Ass wiped. Moving on.

A few months later after talking with Miss Conrad. I had been out riding my Harley with some friends. We had stopped over at the Cafe and we were talking about some of the things that happen around here. I was telling him about the blue glass and the house burning down. Mine and the one which previously sat there.

His eyes got big and he said. "Wow! Two houses? That's some serious hot spot of activity. You know.... Back in the old days, people use to paint their windows blue to ward off evil spirits."

I just looked at my other friend with suspicious curiosity. "No way! That is crazy!"

"It's true. You should google it. You can google anything these days. Information is just a finger tip away."

"I will. That's weird as shit."

So here I set, at my computer and I just googled it. As I'm reading it, I got freaking cold chill's. So I called Mom immediately. "Mom, you got to see the shit I'm reading."

"What are you reading?"

"Shit about the blue glass Miss Conrad was talking about."

She needed no more explanation. "I'll be right over."

She always comes right over when I tell her to, whether she knows what's going on or not. She knows it's gonna be something interesting. When she arrives and gets to the door, I tell her to get her ass up here so I can spill the beans. When she comes up the stairs, I start reading to her. She can't read you know. Ha.. Just kidding.

She is tripping and her curiosity had been peeked. She wants to know more. All of a sudden the front door flew open. Mom about jumped out of her seat.

As I laugh "It's just Amy Mom! She needs money for some bill or something. You know I'm the Raywick Bank around here, I just don't get paid interest. She called me before I called you, and said she was coming over."

Amy yells out, "You biznitchs home?"

"Yes Amy, we're upstairs."

"What the hell ya'll doing up there?"

"We're researching about this blue glass that Conrad's wife told me about."

"What blue glass?"

"Blue glass to keep out ghost."

"Oh! Is Walter at it again?"

"A little, but this shit doesn't have nothing to do with him."

Mom jumps in, "Amy, I believe Crock was right, this ghost is old."

Amy peeked over my shoulder and said. "Is Crock your Ex Missy? The one that always comes over to the Cafe with her big hat and knife strapped on?"

"Yes Amy, that's Crock."

"Well, Missy my mom has a ghost, I swear she does. My son Ben won't stay there, he never has. Missy, you better make sure you talk to your ghost. You know what it is Missy? You stirred up some real shit with that first Halloween party you had. Us doing that *JonBenet Ramsey* shit! That was a big mistake!"

"I know Amy, maybe the barn was their hangout or playground, some crazy shit like that."

"Shut up Missy. I'm getting cold chills." Amy said.

Mom sets straight up in her chair and starts smacking me in my leg. "What about Summer saying that man was standing above her."

"I know, I'm afraid to even be talking about this right now. I'm scared they are listening to us."

Mom nods her head. "Well exactly. You know they are Missy, they're right here silly. Right here with us."

I look around and start to talk into the air. "Well Walter, if it was you that was standing over Summer, I hope you were just looking out for her. Walter! I think maybe you're just here to protect the little slave girl. If you are watching over her, you need to calm her little ass down. She is getting way too rambunctious. She has been here all along hasn't she. I'm with Crock on this one. Are you just watching over her? Can you give me a little sign?"

Mom jumps up and starts to shake the chills off. "Stop! You're scaring me. Your making my hairs stand up and everything. I'm leaving."

As they were both walking down the steps, I made one last comment. "Well ladies, I am about to piece this puzzle together."

Speaking of puzzles. I have a blonde joke for you. It's long, just wait for it.

A blonde called her boyfriend and said, "Please come over here and help me. I have a killer jigsaw puzzle, and I cant figure it out or how to get started." Her boyfriend asked, "what is it supposed to be when its finished" the blonde said, "according to the picture on the box, it's a tiger." Her boyfriend decided to go over and help with the puzzle. She let him in and showed him where she had the puzzle spread all over the table. He studied the pieces for a moment, looked at the box, then turned to her and said, "first of all, no matter what we do, were not gonna be able to assemble these pieces into anything resembling a tiger." he took her hand and said, "second, I want you to relax. Let's have a nice cup of hot chocolate and then........" he sighed,.... "Lets put all these frosted flakes back in the box."

Question: *Is there good and evil in this house, all mixed up together like sweet and sour chicken. The possibilities could be horrendous, or they could be quite amazing, or it could be, just nothing. Just random crazy shit happening in the universe again.*

Before we move on, let me fill you in on the *Ramsey* story. I'm sure we all know who *JonBenet Ramsey* is. It was a terrible tragedy for that little girl and her family. If you don't know the story, google it. This is gonna sound terrible, and quite frankly it is. But while we were setting up for the Halloween party, we were making some pretty realistic harsh scenes. You know, your typical adult horror movie scenes. I had taken stuffing, mask, dolls, mannequins, anything that would help make good scary props. Joe Mack and Nicole started with a little doll. Then they wrote a note to lay beside her. When we started to read the note, we looked up with judgmental eyes. They looked and asked. "Too soon?" We all hesitated then replied, "Nah! It's Halloween, go ahead." And that they did.

Sometimes its too early to make a joke. Comedians deal with this shit all the time. Sometimes they take a chance on it to soon, when trying to comatize a celebrity death. Anytime would be too soon in my book, but that's comedy. *Joan Rivers,* set the bar on this sort of thing and we're all probably going to hell in gasoline panties for that.

Months later after the party, Dad and Jimmy, ended up calling the police. Why you say? They found the note out in the field in the fence line and it was the ransom note. They honest to God thought someone around here had been kidnapped. Everyone was calling

296

around to find out if anyone was missing. Finally, someone called Amy. Then she called me. She was laughing her ass off. "Oh my God, you guys. That's the note we wrote for the party, the Ramsey note. Don't you remember?"

"Oh shit, I do. But I had forgotten all about it, until now!"

Now I'm not saying finding the note, had anything to do with anything. I'm just saying, we set up horrible Halloween props that may have offended our guest, not living guest either! Trying to find out the answers and having the time to do it, is like peeling an endless bag of onions, literally.

So wait a minute, shit! I never told you about the blue glass or why Mom was freaking out. Yes! I googled it. Oohhh! What did I find? I read that the color blue was used to ward off evil spirits. Page after page staring at me. Stories of ghost and the color blue, *haint blue,* to be exact. People painted their porches and their window trims this color blue to keep the haints out, just like my friend had said.

Haints, are what ghost were called in the old, old days. And no, they were not considered to be nice. (definition of a haint; In traditional belief and fiction, a ghost is the soul spirit or spirit of a dead person or animal that can appear, in visible form or other manifestations to the living.)

It is folklore brought in from the South, first used by African slaves. They still believe in this myth down in the South and Charleston. They say there are also spirits. (ones who only show up to comfort you, the kind that would bake you a pie if they could.) The ghost that I have, you know, the one we named Walter, maybe he wasn't a ghost at all. Maybe his spirit stuck around to protect the other spirit or ghost we have, or may not have. I don't think the presence we have is mean or vindictive, just stuck. Maybe he just wants to go home. Maybe he feels like Summer did when she went to Paris when she was only sixteen. She was home sick and just wanted to come home.

Maybe he likes sticking around. Is he protecting us? Is he trying to help the little slave girl cross over. I wanna know! How do I know? How will I ever know? Now I'm feeling a little bit like *Whitney Houston,* How I will I know if he really loves me. Sorry songs really take over my head sometimes.

Back to what I was saying. I am coming to realize and really believe, that maybe, just maybe we really are sharing our space with someone. Not necessarily just the house, but the land. I have broaden my thoughts. It's kinda unbelievable. Maybe this land has a spirit angel and a haint (ghost). Not sure! Ghost can't cross over to find their way. Sometimes they need assistance in fixing something. What do they need fixed? If a spirit can cross over and come back, maybe when Walter died in 1959, he decided to stay and help her. Maybe he has a passport to travel back and fourth.

Summer and her friends have heard the pattering of little feet from time to time. Are they hers while she is playing. Maybe she didn't know how to leave. You must remember slaves were never allowed to leave the grounds of their owners. This was the only place she knew. What do they need? How can I help? These souls need peace, and I need some peace myself. Because I don't feel comfortable doing certain things in my house. I feel like a child or man, or both, is watching me at all times. There is a presence here, I do not doubt that! I am continuously trying to work the puzzle, I am both intrigued and a bit shaken, because I know that nothing is impossible.

They say if you walk through a haint, you can become one when you die. I pray I haven't, I would go stir crazy if I couldn't get someone's attention. I would probably burn a house down too, tip some cows or something. Speaking of cow tipping, does that really exist? I think its an urban legend myself. Maybe I will get the girls at work to go try it.

Anyway, maybe we should name the little girl. Maybe she wants a name, or has a name that we should already be calling her by. I'm sure she is tired of being called *little girl*. Maybe it's not a she at all, maybe its a little boy, if so, he is really gonna be pissed off at us calling him a girl. But for now, we feel it's a little girl. Maybe someday we will have an ultra sound that will be able to tell, technology may be the key. Maybe that's why I've had two sound bars delivered to my door, when I in fact did not purchase them. Maybe they want to communicate and ordered them through my Iphone. I can understand it being a mistake once, but twice? Hell I don't know.

What will I name her? huuummmmm.... Oh! I got it. I think 'May Bee' would be a spectacular name. Yep! That's her name from now on, hope she likes it. People from these parts always seem to have two names. She has to like it.

When I tore out the staircase, did May Bee move to the barn for cover? Is that why the cat hangs out there? Was it May Bee's playground or hideout or maybe her and Walters place to hang to plot and scheme? If it was, we were sure to disturb that with the Halloween party and all. Did we piss them off? I hope the hell not.

With everything that was happening around here, someone or something seems to be pissed off. Was May Bee murdered or killed in some awful fashion? Is there something about the land that lets spirits manifest? What keeps them here? Maybe they have a story that needs to be told.

Did she accidentally burn down the house or were they trying to get our attention? Because we weren't paying attention to their advances, when they turned on the radios and the Dish player, messing with all our electronics. I mean, we were paying no mind to it at all. We were just laughing at the crazy shit, not taking it, or Crock seriously, until the house burned to the ground. Then and only then, the name Walter came into play. The thought of it all kind of hit us like a ton of bricks. But, even then, we continued to joke. Although the knocking on the garage door several times has me curious about their ability to enter that part of the compound. I have never had anything to happen inside the garage.

Miles even recalls a night over there when she was watching a movie with me and something pounded on the door. I don't recall details of it, except we were watching the movie *Quarantine,* but she swears by it.

How come they can't get in there? Is it because the building is new or made of a certain material? The Cafe is made of metal and I've had several workers to tell me that they have felt something over there. I won't ever know until we are able to come in complete contact with the spirit world, until then I will just research and assume, to the best of my knowledge. If you think I'm sounding a little crazy at this point, just know that if you believe in angels, you have to be curious about the lost souls that didn't find their way. We all get lost. Why can't that happen in the after life? Be back soon, got to grab a snack.

INVESTIGATING MY SITUATION

I'm back, It's gonna take me a minute to focus. I just rubbed a freakin red hot potato chip in my eye, and it burns burns burns, like a ring of fire... Like a ring of fire. It sucks when snack time becomes hazardous, but yet, it does all the time.

So today, I finally found some free time. So I headed up to the court house and the library and did a little research. Yes I know! It's hard to picture me in a library. But I'm determined to find out what happened on this ground that produced such a powerful lingering energy. This segment was really hard to figure out.

Keep in mind, I'm no Genealogist, history buff, ghost buster or a hound dog. I can't guarantee I got all the facts straight, cause I'm not a factual person. However, I don't mean that in a way that I don't tell the truth, I just mean facts and dates are no concern to me. I am just trying to establish some kind of timeline. When the lady walked me in the room all I could say was, "Damn! Property books are huge." They looked as big to me as grandma's panties did when I was a kid. I mean freakin huge. They were also hard as hell to read. It was like trying to read the rocks the *Mayans* wrote on. To top it all off, you have to research backwards. Then flip the the fat ass books around and start from the very beginning. Then of course take notes, then come home and report it to you. I'm becoming quite the investigator and reporter, still working on the writer.

So let me tell you what I have learned. There was a cabin on this property back in the seventeen hundreds. It's when this particular land was actually still part of Washington County. I was previously told it belonged to the Millers, whom raised 12 children here, or at least on a nearby knob. Who knows? Back then they documented

301

their land ownership only by big or small sycamore trees. So I'm not sure on the span of the property. I'm almost certain I'm sitting on a smaller piece than the original acres. Well, in fact I have to be.

After their deaths, sometime in the 1840's, it is said that only two of their children stuck around. The couple are believed to be buried somewhere here in the valley. The daughter married a man by the name Peter Abell, whom drowned near Theodore Spalding Bridge, in the Rolling Fork River. That river runs right behind this property, toward Saint Joe. Theodore Spalding Bridge, doesn't exist anymore, it has been gone for many years. What I would like to know. Did they ever find his body?

The son David Miller Jr. Was born in 1799, and was the youngest. He was raised in the log home, which is now long gone, nothing remains but a pile of stone.

He married and had fourteen children himself and seemed a little busy, if you get my drift. Seven boys and seven girls. Two of the boys died at a very young age, plus one girl Martha Ellen died around age nine. Layfayette, died around the age twenty-one.

I don't know what the cause of death was on any of the children. I'm beginning to wonder if they're hanging around knocking on my walls. Psst, I think I may have something. Maybe I should be speaking to Martha Ellen.

All the other children lived to a ripe old age according to certain letters and documents. One being Lucinda, whom married Robert Burdette.

Robert Burdette and his wife Lucinda, pictured above.

They purchased this property in 1904, for 600 dollars. Fact. In 1914 when both Robert and his wife, Lucinda Miller Burdette, passed away, only a month apart, it was then sold to Edward T. Peterson for $5500. I'm thinking the Burdette's had built a home on it, due to the price increase.

In 1916 Edward died in his home of pneumonia and left his estate to his wife Cora Peterson. I don't think Cora lived here, but I do believe their daughter, Josephine Peterson Burdette, lived here in that house, because its been told that the house in which she resided burned down sometime in the thirties. Apparently the one Miss Conrad had told me about. I was also told a story by Josephine's great grandson, that when the house burnt, she left town and never came back.

I'm thinking this lady was afraid of something. Is she the one who had painted the windows blue? If not, how would you explain the blue glass coming up in the yard when Miss Conrad was a kid?

The house burning and the blue glass story is just too much of a coincidence. What and who, was she afraid of?

When I continued searching the records at the courthouse I learned that the land was sold to C.C. Hines in 1934 for a thousand bucks. So I assume there was no house standing, especially with the price drop again, deeming the story to be true. It's interesting as I watch the dots start to connect.

Here's a dot for you, although I can only speculate what actually happened here. It's known that on Halloween 1933, things started spiraling out of control, even in isolated rural areas. Youngsters cruised around in farm trucks, causing mischief and pulling pranks on the local farmers. Things like turning over tractors, putting things on top of their homes, setting fires and opening gates to let the flocks out into the night. Some farmers confronted these youngsters with their Smitty, and the confrontations got bloody.

Question: So was Josephine Peterson Burdette part of someone's prank? Or did it go much deeper than that?

So I drove over to the library to try and find a newspaper article that would show or tell about the fire. But to my surprise, obviously fire wasn't the big news back then. I couldn't locate it. It would have been like trying to find a needle in a hay stack. I most certainly didn't have the patience or time to go through every slide. There were way more stories to be written about than I ever would have imagined. Crimes were daily front page news. Articles like shootings and the murder rate was high as hell. Robberies every day, and even one of the Burdette ladies was going on trial because her husband got shot in the middle of a hold up. I couldn't believe the amount of shootings. I guess Bonnie and Clyde wasn't the only couple out stealing for a living. Someone said they were just plain mean back then. It was during the worst economic depression ever, and they were just using survival skills I guess. Maybe people need to quit putting blame on video games for violence, since there were none back then and focus elsewhere on the problem.

The paper let me know who went to visit who, and who had colds or illnesses leading to death. Which that didn't surprise me much. That seemed to sound quite normal you know. I did watch *Little House on the Prairie. T*here were people always visiting the doctor in that show, falling ill to malaria and all kinds of shit.

Also to my surprise, while scrolling through the newspaper films, lots of car wrecks. I mean they were off the chart. Guess I would have been front page news. They had ads for brand new Chevrolets trucks for sale for eight hundred bucks. Wowsa!

Moving along, and back to more land transfers. On March 17, 1942, this land was purchased by our friend Mr. Walter for $4200. So once again, another house had to be built and most likely built by C.C. Hines. Yes, obviously he built the skeleton key hole house, with two front doors, that I would eventually end up living in.

Walter, was only 53 when he died, and his wife didn't pass for many, many years to follow. She was 70 at the time of her death. At that point I'm assuming she passed the property on to her son J. W. Jarboe in 1967, although she didn't pass till 1976, according to records. Maybe she was trying to avoid the estate tax and trusted her son not to boot her out, which is what some kids would do today. They even kill their parents for the inheritance. Shame! Shame! They for sure weren't concerned with baking their own pie.

My dad purchased this land back in 1994 from J.W. Which is Miss Conrad's brother. Then I purchased the house in 2003 for $21,400. So there! You have it. The paper trail. All that work for couple pages of boring history, but history I needed to know. Just to let you know, part of the paper trail was lost due to the courthouse burning down in 1863. It lost all records dating back to 1834. Why 1834? Because the rest of the records would be logged in at the Washington County Court House, because we were Washington County. That's the year Marion County became the 84th county formed in Kentucky. I sure wasn't driving there for more facts. We don't care, do we?

It's hard to imagine all the life and death that happened here. That's not including even father back. Several wars have directly affected the region. Including the French and Indian War, Revolutionary, Northwest Indian War, Tecumsehs War, War of 1812. What the hell? Never heard of that one. And don't forget the Civil War. Jesus! This country has been at war, ever since Christopher got lost and stepped on this part of the continent. There could be an assortment of souls wondering these grounds causing all the unusual activity. They say unruly deaths enable spirits to walk the earth. Could there be some makeshift graves here? I certainly believe there is.

This land was part of the Revolutionary War dating all the way back to 1775, which didn't end till 1783. How many souls were lost in this area during that brutal war. Back then the British and Indians became allies. They planned an attack at Rudle and Martin Station, which is now known to be Central Kentucky, I think. When the gates opened the Indians rushed in killing the sickly and throwing babies into fires. They scalped many, because they received five dollars from the British for every scalp they took.

Kentucky was also battlegrounds during the Civil War, which was a blood bath. They fought at close range. The soldiers screams had to be deafening. If we listened in history class, which I didn't, we should all know that Kentucky was the border state that tied both the North to the South. Which in return pitted brother against brother

306

when the state decided to stay neutral. By law, Kentucky was still a slave state. Kentucky was the source of slaves for cotton, and slave trade was a profitable business, although most Kentuckians didn't own slaves. Mr. William Bickett did, and lived right across the hill.

In 1861 and 1862 Kentucky saw a number of battles and skirmishes. Even though Confederate forces retreated from the state in 1862, and slaves were to be free in 1863, confederate raids still caused mayhem in the state from then till 1865. They continued to fight about it even after Lincoln declared them free.

"*Bushwhackers*" whom were unruly soldiers, from both sides, took a hold of the land. They looted small towns and robbed farmers. They burned bridges, courthouses and personal property. I'm guessing that maybe our courthouse fell victim to that, when the battle in Lebanon took place July 5, 1863. Just assuming at this point. Have to admit, I didn't look for the facts.

I did a weeks worth of research for three pages. WOW Pawpaw! On with the story.

But Crock is dead set that it's a little black slave girl roaming these parts. For whatever the reason she believes this, I don't know. I'm not sure how evolved her senses are. I just know that she is convinced for whatever reason, that something unnerving happened here, and little May Bee just can't rest.

One day a stream of water was coming up right beside my newly built house, like someone had stuck a water hose up through the ground, just a bubbling spring. I was told there is a natural stream that runs under the house. I had no idea, I guess I should have known this since there was a red water pump that sat in the back yard, just never thought about a stream running into it. I just assumed the

307

previous owners had water brought in with water trucks, like they use to do at my grandma's house. It was plowed over and filled in after the house burnt. Question? Was someone, thrown down in the well? Maybe like, in the movie, *The Ring?* The thought of that, is some scary shit.

Summer and her cousin Josh and the WELL.

We also, already know, that the Rolling Fork winds all around me. During days of the wars even the Indian War, they must have taken cover and refuge on the knobs of the river, picking off intruders that were trying to get to places via water. What does this matter? I don't know. Does any of this relate to Indians? Were they buried here? Were soldiers buried here? Was my little May Bee buried here? Was she Indian, black, white? Doesn't matter to me, I just want her to know. I'm here to help if I can.

It will take a lot more digging to find out the answers and I don't mean just in paper work and stories, actual digging for artifacts. I don't think that's a challenge I want to take on? I would much rather bottle the spring water and retire and move to a cabin.

I think whomever it is, wants me to find out the truth and release them. I don't think they want to be taunting me, just for the fun of it. I'm hoping they are like the spirits in the movie *Ghost*. But either way, it's making me lose sleep at night, and I wish she, they, them, or him, would quit playing with the fire alarm. They have done it twice and I'm done with it. I would set them in the corner if I could get ahold of em and spank their little asses, if they are children. Can't really mess with the big boys.

Here is the thing people. Although I think it's funny and we have comatized the hell out of this situation. I don't wanna joke no more, well, maybe a little bit. But I still want to resolve what's been happening around here. I still feel as if I'm being watched, and I'm not comfortable with that. Would you be? I think not.

Is everything connected? I feel that it is. The land, the presence, the weird stuff. All of this has blown the door wide open to what I believe and don't believe. But I'm still trying to find a reason to lighten things up. Maybe once the answer is revealed everyone can make nice and walk off into the sunset together.

It's just weird, that what I am coming to believe now, is something that I never thought I would believe in. Ghost!!!!! I am sharing my space with something, and it's not alive and breathing, and it sure in the hell isn't a pet, or maybe it is, it could be that too. Especially when I find myself walking over to the Cafe. Then I hear panting behind me and stop! Look back! Nothing is there, absolutely nothing. Freakin weird I say.

Spirits have always been said to be the natural environment of our world, from the beginning of time. Depending on what we are willing to accept or get a glimpse of.

Does this land really have a spirit angel and a haint ghost? I'm still not sure!! But you can bet your ass, that when the fire alarm went off at 3:13 in the morning a few nights ago, while I was lying alone asleep on the couch, the possibility increased in my mind.

I was shocked right out of my sleep into complete alertness. I ran straight to the kitchen, only to realize it was the fire alarm upstairs. I ran toward the steps and as soon as I grabbed the railing to run up, it stopped in an instant. It went from blaring to complete silence. Ghost? Hell yes...what else was it? I couldn't get back to sleep and had the heebie-jeebies the rest of the night and no one there to give a shit. At least it is kinda funny, when you have guest who get scared out of their skin. They put their head under blankets, like that's gonna do em some good. You know them suckers can crawl right up in there with you, if they want to. BOO!

So early that morning I called Jo Eddie and asked him what would make an alarm go off. He paused for a moment. "Hum, I don't know Missy, maybe heat or steam coming from the shower."

I sarcastically stated. "Jo Eddie, it was three something in the morning, really!"

"Well, Missy, it must have been some kinda of motion or heat coming from the walls or something."

"Yes of course, I know this. Some kind of interference." I'm thinking duh! A ghost. But he didn't catch on, so I just ended the conversation and went about my hectic day as usual and pushing it to the back of my brain storage till another day. And no! The batteries weren't low. They were perfectly good. Even if they were bad, it wouldn't matter. Because one night a friend was here, the alarm started beeping. Not blaring, but, the kind of beep, when batteries are low. It was getting on our nerves, so we took the battery out and it decided to beep at us once more, just for good measures. Kinda like, ugh! In your face!

REAL TIME: RIGHT NOW AT THIS VERY MOMENT.

Okay Readers, I'm sitting here at the computer. I'm gonna tell you a story that just happened this very instant. I just wanted to tie up this story. With what kind of ending, I'm not quite sure. But once again, it has turned into, what the hell is going on moment.

I just recently decided I wanted to try and quit smoking. So I bought me a *Blu Cig,* you know the electronic one? The ones that when you suck in, it makes a noise and the end turns blue. It only sends out nicotine vapors. Well, my friends, I just took a draw and it was somewhat nasty. Then I was sitting here, relaxing and thinking. I was holding it in my hand, left hand to be exact, not that that matters, just a fact. When all of a sudden it started to make its noise and the end turned blue. I thought it was about to blow up in my hand, so I tossed it. I didn't know what was going on. But oh! I do know what's going on! Something just took a fucking drag off it.

I'm gonna have to ask Miss Conrad if her dad smoked, I don't know how I'm gonna go about asking this question to her, without making myself sound like a crazy person. I probably already sound like one to you. But I'm just stating the facts...

What's the plan? What will I do? I decided to call Amy instead. She had already given me Patty Starr's number months ago. (Patty is a well known ghost chaser.) I didn't want to call, cause sometimes there is a reason for this silly shit. But at this point I'm being bombarded with things that just aren't adding up. So if it's not a ghost, I sure in the hell, have some really messed up energy following me around. Wait!!! That is a ghost. Energy is ghost, energy with no, body. But once again, whose? It could be anybody, or no-body.

Maybe first, I should google and check to see if these type of cigs have ever backfired before. Especially, before I go calling out a culprit. I don't wanna be looking like a fool or some loony tune, that belongs in a nut house. Be right back with an answer.

Found it, not really an answer we were looking for. One of these cigs blew up in a man's mouth. But I only found one incident and the article said it was reported, that the situation was suspicious. Don't think it has any relation to what just happened here, AT ALL. Maybe it did, maybe he has a Ghost, who likes them too. Ghost are just like magic, something we don't understand. Therefore, it is way and above us. Patty Starr, here I come.

"I wanted the perfect ending. Now I've learned the hard way, that some poems don't rhyme, and some stories don't have a clear beginning, middle and end. Life is about not knowing, having to change, taking the moment and making the best of it, without knowing what's going to happen next. Delicious Ambiguity. --Gilda Radner—

In closing:

Once again, I would like to thank all my readers for purchasing or downloading my book. I'm hoping you all enjoyed it. I once again apologize for the salty language. It's something that just comes with e territory around here.

I have high hopes on getting my third edition out a little quicker than this one, but like I always say, life gets in the way.

I learn something new about writing every day. Especially when I read someone else's work or when someone reads over mine. I'm just glad I moved up from my humble beginning when I first started writing, when it was more like See Spot Run. You Tarzan me Jane kind of writing. Well, that's what Susan Spicer said. Hope you all agree.

I would like to thank Susan Spicer for reading over my final work. We both realize there is no such thing as perfection, so I hope nothing too big stuck out. Also, I would like to thank Summer for the painting on my cover once again. Nicole, I halfway thank you for reading halfway through, I totally understand. You know I know, that life gets in the way. Beverly, I thank you for reading through it the first time, but since you know the family, I understand why you didn't catch any of my mistakes. The adult mind does that. Like on the Internet, when it has a paragraph that looks like mumble jumble, but we still can read it. "I cdnuolt blveiee taht I cluod aulacity uesdnatnrd what I was rsandieg." And yes, that is what my book looks like first draft, because I type as if I'm dyslexic.